A MEMOIR

Shitfaced

Musings of a Former Drunk

Seamus Kirst

Dear Kate,

Thank you so much for your support for this project! It is much appreciated.

♡

Seamus

Seamus Kirst/CreateSpace
4900 LaCross Road
North Charleston, SC 29406
www.seamuskirst.com

Publisher's Note: While this is a work of nonfiction, I acknowledge that it is my recollection of events. I relate the events to the best of my knowledge. Unless consent was given, some names, and unnecessary identifying characteristics were changed. Actual locales and public names are sometimes used for atmospheric purposes.

Book Layout © 2017 BookDesignTemplates.com

Shitfaced: Musings of a Former Drunk/ Seamus Kirst. -- 1st ed.
ISBN 978-0692822814

In memory of Dr. Donna Wick, a wonderful friend, a beautiful person and an inspiration in fighting to destigmatize mental illness and addiction.

To anyone whom needs a warm hug or a swift kick in the ass: I hope you find both within the pages of this book.

I wanted to write about everything, the life we're having and the lives we might have had. I wanted to write about all the ways we might have died.

— MICHAEL CUNNINGHAM, *THE HOURS*

Author's Note

The bulk of this book details some of the more disturbing moments of my struggle with substance abuse. It does not include many nights that were 'fun;' nights where I convinced myself my drinking was 'fine' or 'normal' or 'under control.'

But, I did have many of those nights. Those nights served as the fuel that allowed me to continually convince myself that I did not have a drinking problem; those nights allowed me to believe that I did not need to stop drinking alcohol and abusing drugs.

If you are struggling with substance abuse, it does not matter how many 'good nights' you have scattered amongst your 'bad nights;' it only takes one bad night to screw up your relationship, to end a friendship, to get a DUI, to get arrested or to die.

If you feel out of control, then listen to yourself. If someone tells you that they are worried about you, then listen to them. People don't tell you they are worried about you because they don't care about you, they tell you that because they care so deeply they cannot stay silent.

If you're deep within your suffering, it may seem like there will not be a life beyond alcohol, or that a dry life will somehow be less fulfilling or exciting. This idea could not be further from the truth: Beyond the alcohol, the drugs, the eating disorder, or whatever else you are struggling with, there is the real you, waiting to be found.

You can get to that place. If you don't know how, ask for help. Talk to someone you trust whether it's a family member, a teacher, a doctor, a therapist or a social worker.

There are people who want to help you.

Please let them help you.

Please help them help you.

Please help yourself.

With love,

Seamus

Foreword by Sean Kirst

I did not say much to my children about alcohol as they were growing up.

Looking back on it, that choice was no mystery.

Maybe if I had – and if I had done it right – Seamus, my oldest son, would never have felt the need to write this book.

But I was good, highly skilled, at running away from who I was. My daughter and two sons would sometimes see me sloppy, but rarely in the state that my friends and I liked to call "wasted." Typically, the kids were already in bed on the nights when I'd start drinking and then wouldn't stop, the nights when I'd think I was the funniest and sharpest guy in the bar and would suddenly be slurring family secrets to total strangers, the nights when I'd turn into a grotesque caricature of myself and wake up in the morning, sick with nausea and diarrhea, the sweat in my hands stinking of alcohol, humiliated at what I remembered ....

If I remembered.

I was a binge drinker, a blackout drinker. I could go weeks without drinking, feeling no need for a drink, which helped me to keep telling myself the big lie: I was not an alcoholic. At worst, I was a "problem drinker," which to me always meant I was free to keep on drinking. An alcoholic, I told myself, needed to drink, and I didn't need to drink .... even if it was only while I was drinking that I would feel good about myself, even briefly, even if drinking was the thing that helped me set aside the sense of shame and self-loathing and inadequacy I'd carried since childhood.

My mother had always been terrified by drinking. It blew apart her immigrant family when she was a child. Her father, an alcoholic, abandoned his children when my mom was small. One of her brothers, a combat veteran of World War II who suffered from post-traumatic shock, killed himself when he was drunk. I was the youngest, and fear of my mother's temper and random violence – she would be waiting, trembling with anger, when you came home late at night - caused me to stay away from alcohol until it seemed as if all my high school friends were getting hammered (they weren't), and the ones who drank the most had the prettiest girlfriends (not always), and I was a guy with thick glasses and rampant acne who wanted to be a star athlete (this was true) as my older brothers and sister had been, and I wasn't even close ....

So I became a star drinker. At a party at 16, maybe the second time I ever touched alcohol, I drank until I was crawling around the floor, drank until my friends carried me home and I became unconscious, drank until my parents took me to the hospital and I woke up sick and ashamed, vomiting over the side of a hospital bed ....

And before long, resumed drinking.

No, my kids did not see much of my actual drinking as they grew up. But they grew up with a drinker, and the sickness that went with it. They grew up with a guy who'd sometimes watch them from the couch while leveled by the headaches and sweats and run-to-the-bathroom sickness of hangovers. They grew up with a guy who believed that any good thing in life demanded a reward – rather than the good thing being a reward unto itself – and that the reward was usually getting wasted. They grew up with a drunk, a guy who sometimes went out at night and did things and said things so embarrassing, so humiliating, so dangerous, it is difficult for me to sit and write these words, because I'm forced to remember and accept what I was.

My drinking was symptomatic. It was tied to a screwball childhood, and a brilliant but wounded and abusive mother, and an utter lack of self-esteem, and – absolutely – to depression, to a struggle with anxiety and mental illness. All the things that drove me to be a writer also led to self-hatred, to an inability to find myself amid the whole, forces that all remain in play to this day. They are part of the journey to wherever this all leads, except for one thing:

I stopped drinking.

I stopped drinking in 2005. I remember the night. I had just won a journalism award that meant something to me, and we went out to celebrate, because I needed the reward; once drunk, I could tell myself how cool and great I was. I was in a downtown bar crowded with cops and prosecutors, on a day when they had just won a high-profile conviction. Many were people I liked, people I'd known for years, but up and down the bar were car keys, stacked like little cairns, monuments to hypocrisy as men and women of the law prepared to join men and women of the press in driving home, utterly wasted. Everyone was getting hammered, sloppy, some not so far from blind drunk, an ancient tradition of both profession. I was just getting started. I stood at the bar with a beer in my hand and I thought about the kids waiting for me at home. I thought about the messages we implant, how we say not to drive drunk and then we do, and how people die because of it – either at once, or bit by bit. I thought about friends I knew in childhood, brilliant friends who could have done amazing things but instead died terrible deaths when they were drunk, friends who were exactly like me.

Or my children.

Just like that, like a wall washed down by a flood, it was over.

I was tired of it all. My hangovers had been getting worse. I got drunk, embarrassingly drunk, more quickly than ever. Two fast beers and my speech would start to slur, and my angry wife would need to ask me to leave a party. Standing in that bar, a cascade of revulsion and fatigue swept me up, and I set down the half-finished beer and left. That was it. No more. I turned to friends in the recovery community, and they strengthened the decision while it was fresh, allowing the mold to harden, and I stopped. I was ready. My drinking came to an end.

Just as my son's was really gaining speed.

I wish now. I wish now. I wish now. I wish now I could do 10,000 things again. I had stopped drinking, but my journey was only beginning. The word 'recovery' is cliché, but it is true. You are never truly beyond drinking. You are always recovering, because drinking never truly leaves the alcoholic DNA. I feel it now, like a presence at the table. The only difference is I'm comfortable to make it sit there, starving. It comes from and draws upon our wounds and flaws, and to be without wounds and flaws is to be divine, which none of us are. Which I will never be. I am always in recovery, exposed to what I am, where my greatest risk must also be a strength.

Seamus was struggling. Our connection had always been both unbearably intense and somehow distant, wary circling, understanding each other all too well and thus piling on lies. In the way of so many wide-open, bright and sensitive little kids, Seamus compensated as he began to learn the world by becoming a wiseass, a very good and astute one, and also by becoming far more guarded, qualities that led him to essentially shut us out once he reached the storm years of adolescence. If there is one memory I would call upon for comfort at that time, it was from 1991 or so, when we were living in a battered flat in Syracuse in a student neighborhood. Seamus would wake up at 3 or 4 a.m. He was maybe 11-months-old, and I would put him in one of those little plastic strollers and walk up and down Fellows Avenue in the middle of the night, both of us wide awake, neither of us speaking, the trees whispering around us, my little boy looking from side to side, observing the quiet city ....

Just utterly content.

Years later, the night I realized it had gone over the brink was the night one of his friend's mothers called the house, trying to cover for him, saying Seamus was a "little drunk" and wanting to know if he could "sleep over." Here is one lesson for any of you who are parents: If we had agreed, Seamus might be dead. Something told us we need-ed to go to that house, where the woman and her daughter dragged Seamus to the stoop, where this kid of 15 fell unconscious on the ce-ment and rolled down the steps. Unconscious drunks are a joke in our culture, until it is your son, alabaster skin, lifeless, everything limp, his head slamming each step as he rolls toward the ground.

He spent the night in the hospital, his blood alcohol level – hours after he stopped drinking - right around .30, and the arc that would become this book began. My initial reaction to my son's excess was to try and be my parents, or more exactly my mother, to punish and shame it out of him, to grind it out of him, to lecture and hector it out of him, to do everything but look at the burning core I should have known and felt, to realize beneath all his noise and anger he was suf-fering. Suffering relentlessly. It took me awhile, a long time, to get to that place. I was late. By the time I found my way to where he was, everything was at high and terrifying risk.

Thinking back on it, I know my wife and I were half-prepared for the worst kind of call in the middle of the night. Nora, too, had grown up in a family torn apart by alcoholism; for her, there was nothing but scar tissue in reliving all those patterns. We did not know if Seamus could ever come back from his addictions. We had seen people lost, people we loved who never found their way. You are about to read his own brave and painfully honest account of those years, but I can tell you that the day when Seamus, too, grew weary and had enough – the day when he stopped drinking - was not the greatest moment in our lives, because there were many days that he stopped, and it didn't last.

The greatest day is right now, as it goes on.

- *Sean Kirst, January 2017, Syracuse, N.Y.*

Introduction

On the two-year anniversary of my decision to give up drinking – a few weeks before I turned 25 – I wrote my essay, 'There and Back Again: Why I Stopped Drinking at 22.' Not thinking much of it, I posted the piece on my blog – a simple website that had previously hardly gotten any traction.

I linked the essay to my Facebook page, and it immediately took off. First, thousands of people shared it around the country. Then the piece went on to be republished on sites including *Advocate.com*, *UpWorthy* and *The Huffington Post*.

The piece continued on to be shared and republished around the world; it was picked up by a site in India, and was even translated into Mandarin and shared on a site in Taiwan.

I was blown away by how many people could relate to my experiences of self-destruction. This essay exposed the moments that had always made me feel so isolated; these were feelings that I'd always worked so hard to forget about and hide. Yet, countless people reached out to me to say my story had resonated with them in some way.

I was even more shocked at how much better I continued to feel as I kept writing about my struggles with addiction and mental illness. In sifting through my darkest moments, and trying to better understand my suffering, I began to actually process my own experiences. The more I broke down the past, the easier it was for me to keep moving forward. In trying to understand the nature of my own mental illness, I started to feel relief; I started to forgive myself, and I began to feel more whole.

I kept writing, and so this project began.

Here is the original essay:

There and Back Again: Why I Stopped Drinking at 22

Two years ago, when I was 22, I decided to stop drinking. Considering my history, the decision happened after a rather insignificant night.

It did not happen the morning I woke up in the hospital with hypothermia and alcohol poisoning.

It did not happen when I spent 30 days in rehab after getting into a drunken fight with my parents and chugging a bottle of mouthwash and a handful of prescription pills.

It did not happen after a 50-something-year-old bartender told me I needed to kiss him to get my ID back, which somehow led to me bringing him back to my dorm and upon realizing I regretted the decision, pretending to be passed out as he pressed his naked body against mine and repeatedly whispered "Don't fall asleep on me, babe."

It did not happen after I had to run away from a homeless man who led me to a park and exposed himself to me after I asked him for directions in Providence.

It did not happen after I almost left a New Delhi Men's Fashion week party with a man who said he was a model but was actually a pimp and hours later texted me, trying to sell me an hour in a limo with a boy or girl for $400.

It happened after what was, for me, a rather routine, if not tame, night: I went out drinking with my friends, blacked out and had to be brought home.

When I woke up in the morning, I felt like I was reaching the surface of water just as I was about to use my last breath of oxygen. I had been so consumed by self-created chaos that I had not had clarity of mind for years.

"What if my friends hadn't been there?" I asked myself. "What if they hadn't brought me home?"

Of course, I already knew the answer, but for the first time I allowed myself to let it sink in: If I didn't stop drinking I was going to wind up taking my life, either intentionally or accidentally.

And it was going to happen soon.

I had been drinking regularly since I was 15. Yet the issue with high school and college drinking is the blurry line between typical — if dangerous — experimentation and blatant drinking problems. It wasn't that bizarre that I hid a bottle of vodka beneath the floorboards in my parent's attic, but I crossed beyond standard teenage rebellion when I'd pour vodka in my mug full of Sprite as a I did my homework.

As a gay teenager in an inner city high school, alcohol took on an extra significance. Drinking is the great equalizer; anyone can do it. Though I loved my close friends, I always felt different — apart. I used alcohol as a means to bond with classmates with whom I otherwise had nothing in common.

In retrospect, the truth was glaring and obvious. By the time I graduated from high school, I had been hospitalized three times for alcohol poisoning, completed a month-long stint in rehab and spent a night in a psychiatric center after a drug-induced breakdown.

After going to rehab — in my sophomore year of high school – I stayed sober for a few months while I completed an outpatient program, but my heart was not in it. I was convinced that I did not have a problem. After each hospitalization, I would have a window of time where I essentially "grounded" myself from alcohol, but within a few weeks I would lie to my parents and find my way back out.

I made myself a victim. When people tried to talk to me about my behavior, whether it was adults or friends, I would lie and if they kept pushing, then cry.

My biggest blessing and curse in high school was that I was able to achieve despite all of my struggles. I was the valedictorian of my class and was accepted at Brown University.

I left for college with high hopes. I wanted to study International Relations and become a human rights lawyer. But without the structure of high school, I quickly fell apart; I drank almost every night.

Where I had been admired for my work ethic in high school, in college I schemed to do the bare minimum.

Though my grades were lower than high school, they were strong enough that I was able to maintain a façade of being okay. I ignored the changes happening to me. I no longer took any joy out of learning, or any joy out of much anything at all, besides partying.

I hid my past from my friends at Brown, but as time went on my troubling relationship with substances came to the surface. By the time I graduated, I had been hospitalized an additional time after an alcohol and cocaine binge and suffered from a Xanax addiction. I'd black out a few times a week. I was aggressive and reckless. I constantly started fights I couldn't remember, both with friends and strangers.

When I wasn't drunk, I was hungover. My anxiety was through the roof. I had trouble sleeping, and would take whatever I could get, whether it was NyQuil, Ambien or Vicodin, just to get through the night.

After college, I moved to New York without a job. My low point: After drunkenly breaking up with my ex-boyfriend at a party, I tried to run into heavy New York traffic while two friends walked me home. They pulled me back. I was in a complete blackout. They tell me I sobbed for an hour and passed out. I awoke the next day at 2 p.m., completely disoriented, and I barely remembered anything from the night before. I stopped drinking for a few weeks, and sulked that I had to. Within the month, I decided I was going to try drinking again with strict rules in place. I would drink only during the weekend and would have no more than three drinks spread out throughout the night.

Needless to say, I was soon drinking during the week and blacking out routinely on weekends. And so on the Sunday morning of the second weekend, I woke up and decided that the only way I might ever be happy is if I never drank again.

If you're a heavy drinker, that decision can seem impossible. I always ran with a hard-partying crowd. For someone young, the thought of losing access to the social situation they've always known is terrifying. Whenever I would try to become sober — which happened at least ten times before it actually worked – the voice inside my head would incessantly shout: *What if I'm less funny when I'm sober? What am I even going to talk to this person about if I'm not drunk? I can't dance until I've taken a few shots! Sleeping with someone without alcohol?!*

I told myself that drinking is what made my world feel magical. My first couple of drinks gave me manic energy and a sweeping sense of happiness, and I would spend the rest of the night trying to not only maintain that feeling, but to make it grow. I remember sitting at my kitchen table during senior week at Brown. It was around noon and I was incredibly hungover. I felt completely flat and empty but as soon as I chugged a beer I came back to life. My depression temporarily subsided and I was bubbly and talkative and vivacious. I gleefully proclaimed, "Wow! I love drinking!" I was convinced I'd lose my true self if I gave up alcohol, because at that point it was rare that I felt happy when I wasn't drunk.

Alcohol felt like my lifeline, and it was only on rare occasions – during common morning panic attacks – that I might even briefly acknowledge that it was actually destroying my life.

One minute I would be drinking and dancing with my friends at the bar and then my next moment of worldly awareness would be when I woke up completely disoriented, panicked, unsure of where I was. Whether I found myself in my dorm basement in my underwear, naked in someone's bed or on a beach in Costa Rica missing my shoes and a wallet, I was never really that shocked.

More times than I would care to admit, I woke up in a pool of my own urine or with vomit splattered against the walls as my phone repeatedly rang or a concerned friend pounded on my door. I often didn't ask questions about what happened the night before, because I didn't want to know the answers.

For me to admit that I did not remember the insults I hurled, or that I did not mean what I had said, would have meant acknowledging that I was out of control.

For me to admit that the sexual situations I found myself in were scary or shameful would have meant reevaluating my own habits and addictions.

Alcoholism has taught me that you really can convince yourself of anything. Instead of recognizing that I needed help, I convinced myself that my outlandish behavior was what made me interesting. Deflection was my weapon of choice. If I woke up frightened, I would tell the story for a laugh. Though people would occasionally confront me, most acted as if I were entertaining. Besides, I quickly realized, if my "partying" pushed a friend away, there were always five more people who wouldn't notice, or frankly care, how many drinks I had or how drunk I got so long as they didn't have to physically carry me home.

It was only two years ago that I was finally able to admit to those I loved — but most important to myself — that drinking wasn't worth it if I would one day wake up seriously hurt.

If I woke up at all.

Learning to live a sober life, in many ways, has been like trying to walk when you're used to crawling. I still remember how easy it was to drink and how much more effort it has taken for me to reach an emotional place where I'm strong enough to choose against it. Besides, whatever problems or feelings I would drink to escape came back, tenfold, the morning after.

For me, the hardest part of sobriety has been learning to be comfortable with myself all of the time. Every day, it gets a little easier. I've had to teach myself how to communicate thoughtfully without poisoning my speech with the fury of alcohol. I have had to learn how to flirt and pursue romance without being a histrionic drunk, lacking both grace and inhibitions.

I understand I have a long way to travel before I achieve self-acceptance or real serenity. But what I do have, finally, is the peace of mind of knowing that I can wake up every morning remembering all that I did the night before – for better or worse – and knowing, in the end, I will be okay.

{ 1 }

Childhood

My childhood was full of ghosts.

No, I am not confessing, "I see dead people;" I did not spend my free time communicating with nebulous apparitions of the dearly departed.

But, my city, my family, my schools all felt like they were haunted; unable to move forward because they were so transfixed on what they had lost; their gazes were locked upon the past.

I grew up in Syracuse, a post-industrial city that's landlocked right smack in the middle of upstate New York. Geographically, central New York is beautiful. There are the Finger Lakes, densely forested rolling hills and apple orchards that overlook deep valleys.

But while growing up in the 90s, Syracuse never culturally felt like the right place for me. Syracuse seemed to suffer from symptoms that are characteristic of many Rust Belt cities; it always felt like a city that could not help but to bitterly remember what it once was, instead of reaching toward what it could be; it always felt like a city that was in crippling mourning.

As industry left and died, the people of the city did not embrace the changes. They acted like everything was staying the same, and could best be described as practicing "shoot yourself in the foot politics." Essentially, any bad urban planning decision you can imagine,

Syracuse had made. Highways bisect its downtown, disconnecting Syracuse University from the business district; Onondaga Lake was the most polluted lake in the world until recently; the city is near the top of national lists for "hypersegregation," meaning most people of color are squeezed into a few small struggling neighborhoods - and another recent study claims Syracuse has the worst extremes of concentrated poverty for Black and Latino populations of the largest 100 cities in the nation.

**

My parents were always broke.

By the time I was old enough to begin remembering, the credit card debt was the black cloud that hung above our heads. But, even still, my parents, especially my mom, had trouble saying "no" to the material requests of my siblings or myself.

She wanted us to have the happy childhood she had been denied by her alcoholic parents.

**

I am always fascinated by how directly correlated a child's anxieties are to their parents' shortcomings. Except, when you're little, you can't comprehend that your parents might even have shortcomings, so instead you fear the invisible force in the world that has pigeonholed your champions in this position of distress.

"Don't answer that," my parents would say when the house phone rang. "It's probably a bill collector."

We lived in one-floor apartments and eventually small houses, where raised voices reached every corner; I would hear them fighting at night about irresponsible spending and about debt.

I loved my parents, but from a young age realized there were many ways that they were out of control, floating along in the world instead of commanding it. I swore to myself I would never be like them in that way.

I didn't want debt; I didn't want to be scared to answer the phone. So I promised myself to always have enough money, I swore I would do whatever it took to be rich enough to not have to constantly be afraid that the bottom might soon fall out.

As a child, I compulsively searched the house for loose change. I scoured near the washing machine and beneath couch cushions, and hung on to money tightly whenever I was given some in birthday cards. At night, while my parents fought about finances in the room next door, I would empty my piggy bank and put the coins into piles on the floor.

Then I counted; I counted once, twice, three times to make sure I knew the exact amount.

It made me feel secure to have these hidden stashes. Control, a fleeting feeling I would fight to maintain.

{ 2 }

A Boy, a Barbie and Shame

When I think back to childhood, I think of shame.

For as far back as I can remember, I always knew I was different. I preferred a Barbie to a ball. Having a sister who is less than a year older than me made access simple and infinite.

Being born in 1990 in a post-industrial, blue-collar environment, gender-neutral parenting had not caught on yet; if it had, it was sure as hell not in Syracuse. I'm pretty sure it still isn't.

Tonka trucks, baseballs and NERF guns were for boys. Barbies, Easy-Bake ovens and jump ropes were for girls. Boys should play football in the street; girls should go to ballet class.

This was well before I'd heard of the gender-based wage inequality, menstrual cycles and perineal tears during birth, and I couldn't help but feel that girls had gotten the better end of the stick.

I was stubborn and unwavering. Having access to my sister Sarah's "girl" toys wasn't enough; I wanted my own. I had post-hippie parents. My dad was a thoughtful, well-liked writer, an artist really, who spent half his days with his head in the clouds, and my mom was a social worker. Her rough childhood with alcoholic parents made her committed to ensuring our days of youth were more joyous.

So, it was not hard to convince my parents that, though I had an X and a Y chromosome and penis between my legs, I, too, needed dolls to be happy. If my parents ever tried to dissuade me, I certainly don't recall.

Our house was a democracy; moving forward, I was indulged. When Sarah got a Barbie, I got one, too. When Sarah got Samantha from the American Girls doll catalogue, I got Molly.

If anything, I took the doll obsession a step further than my sister. I read all of the American Girl doll books. I had small scale Cinderella and Beauty and the Beast castles in my bedroom; I spent hours moving the almost microscopic characters around the castle grounds, lost in my own dreams that one day, like Snow White and Cinderella, I too would find a romantic partner who would provide me with immeasurable wealth, incomparable real estate and unending emotional validation.

***

My little brother was always such a boy, in the traditional sense. His first word was "ball." He was a natural athlete, excelling at baseball, basketball and football from the time he could walk.

Every year, for birthdays and holidays, I would ask for dolls or princess castles, and most every year, that was what I was given.

It was an act of rebellion. I saw how grown men looked at my presents, and my stomach would tense as I would be overcome with embarrassment; I would want to cry. I could have just waited to get them at home on my birthday or Christmas morning, in the privacy and safety of my immediate family. But, something within me wanted to protest societal expectations.

Why shouldn't I be able to get a new princess castle? Why should I have to hide it?

I kept asking to get those presents, and my parents – whom I'm sure could see the reactions of other adults, just as well as I did – kept giving them.

5

***

As I grew older, the rebellious spirit within me died down; I became more self-conscious about playing with "girl toys."

You get so sick of hearing, "Why do you talk like a girl?" - so you make conscious efforts to deepen your voice, to not let your sentences go up at the end.

You get so sick of hearing, "Why do you walk like a girl?" - so you make sure your hips aren't switching, you walk slower, more controlled.

You get so sick of hearing, "Why are you playing with girls' toys?" - so you just start doing it out of sight, on your own, secretly.

Other children vocalize their opinions, their preconceived notions and expectations as to what you should be, how you should behave. Adults are subtler, their judgment more discreetly implied. I was so tuned into quiet, even unspoken, adult opinions.

I wanted their approval. I wanted everyone's approval.

So, when visible, I morphed myself into what they wanted me to be; what I thought I should be.

***

My favorite Barbie was "Holiday Princess Belle," the doll based on Disney's "Beauty and the Beast: The Enchanted Christmas" – a VHS I also owned and loved. Belle came with a dark maroon lip and a velvet ball gown with gold detailing. I played with her all the time.

I eventually grew tired of her extravagant ball gown, and switched her to a cloth blue dress that I bought from Amish people at a farmer's market. When I played with her I would hold her by the hair and spin her so the skirt of her bucolic gown ballooned out. I did this so often that her hair began coming off, revealing small bald spots. Luscious locks or receding hairline, I still loved her just the same.

For a while, Sarah, Liam and I all lived in the same room, filled with all of our toys. When Sarah moved across the hall to her own room, I let her take most of the dolls - and the trunk we kept filled with Barbies and their accessories - with her.

The bunk bed that I used to share with Sarah became just my own. I moved from the top bunk to the bottom, and I filled the former with a huge pile of stuffed animals.

Stuffed animals are for boys and girls, so those are fine. I can let those show.

Unbeknownst to anyone but me, I kept Belle on the top bunk, buried beneath the stuffed animals. I always knew exactly where she was.

Today she is under the Pikachu, next to the Mickey, just above the Tweety.

***

I am ashamed.

By then, I was in second grade. I had been made more than well aware of what was boxed off as being made for girls and what was fair game to be used by boys. I was getting older and still wanted to play with a Barbie. An intense secretiveness shrouded my time with Belle. Sarah had mostly stopped playing with Barbies, and I announced to my parents that I had, too. It was time for me to grow up.

But, in my heart, all I wanted to do was play with Belle.

***

One morning, before school, I thought I was upstairs alone. I sat on my bed, humming and twirling Belle by her hair.

I heard a rustling in the hall. My heart dropped. I peered out.

Who is that?

The door to my room started creaking open, and I quickly tried to stash Belle in between the bed and the wall. It was too late. My mom had seen me.

"Honey, I saw you playing with that Barbie," she said. "Why do you feel like you have to hide it?"

I had been tranquil just a moment before. I immediately burst into tears, the kind of uncontrollable sobbing where you can't even form a sentence.

"I d-d-d-on't... I d-d-d-on't want to talk about it," I cried. "Why were you spying on me? Can't you just pretend you didn't see?"

"I wasn't spying on you. I could see into your room as I walked up the stairs," she explained softly. "Why are you so upset?"

"I know it's a girl toy," I said. " Sometimes I just wish I had been born a girl; my life would be so much easier."

"Do you think you are a girl on the inside?" she asked gently, concerned.

"NO!" I shouted. "I want to play with girls' toys, but I don't want to be a girl!"

I continued to cry harder and harder; I was having a panic attack, an identity crisis. I couldn't wrap my head around why everything and everyone has to stay so tightly boxed-in.

She started crying too.

"I'm sorry," she whispered. "I was just trying to help."

***

With my room no longer feeling like a safe space, I began hiding Belle even deeper amongst the jumbled heap of stuffed animals.

After careful scouting to absolutely make sure no one was proximate or observing, I would pull her out and stuff her into my armpit, shielding her beneath my billowy t-shirt. I would lock her head into my sweaty crevice and quickly creep to the bathroom. I would lock the door and play with her without anyone watching.

I took Belle into the bath with me, letting her stand beneath the spout as I imagined it was some beautiful waterfall in the fantasyland that I created for her in my mind.

Afterwards, I would towel her off, stick her back into my armpit and bring her back to my room where I put her back beneath my stuffed animals.

***

8

This secret playing went on for months. Then, one day, I heard my mom say hi from outside of the bathroom. I was taking a bath and thought I was home alone and had forgotten to bring anything in besides a towel.

Where can I hide her where no one can see? Can I keep her beneath between my thighs and still walk normally? No. Can I hide her in here?

Our bathroom was rather small, and there was not a hiding spot where I didn't fear my mom might see her again. I really didn't want to have to have another conversation about why I was secretive about Belle. Even if she didn't bring it up, I hated that sense of awareness that there was something another person wanted to talk to you about; that it was in their mind and on the tip of their tongue.

I had a plan.

"I'll be right out!" I shouted to my mom. I took Belle and brought her over to the roll of toilet paper. I began slowly unrolling it and wrapping her up; I mummified her. *What better disguise?* When I was done, I emptied the wastebasket and jammed her into the bottom. I covered her with the empty toilet paper rolls that had been sitting there from before.

I flushed the toilet washed my hands and scurried out.

***

That afternoon, I got distracted playing Sega. An hour passed, and I suddenly remembered Belle.

I darted up the stairs to the wastebasket. It was empty!

I hurried downstairs to check the kitchen trashcan. It was empty too! The trash had been brought outside.

I opened the back door and sprinted across the yard to where the garbage cans were lined up in between the garage and the fence.

There were four garbage cans, and they were all filled near to the brim with giant white trash bags.

I can rummage through these, I thought. *I can find Belle. I can save her.*

But something within me made me hold back.

No, I thought. *It's over; Belle's gone.*

I turned around and walked back to the house. I felt like I had lost a friend, but sometimes losing a friend can also be a relief. I didn't get to say goodbye, but in a way I did.

Did I mean to hide her, or did I mean to throw her out?

I mummified her and put her in the wastebasket. I disposed of her like trash, and like trash she was taken away to rot in some landfill.

Well, actually, she was plastic, so like the dog toys in the bushes that were still there after Autumn had passed, I knew she might not ever rot. She'd rather just sit there forever, melting beneath the summer sun's glare, and becoming ever frigid in the winter's biting winds. Fading from the light, the rain, and the melting snow. She would become just a faceless, balding, piece of plastic.

That was her fate, the fate I had delivered to her. Should I feel guilty now? Should I feel guilty that it felt like a weight had been lifted?

Should I feel sorry for her, or should I feel sorry for me? Should I feel sorry that Belle was now just a part of my past?

{ 3 }

Unwell

My first memory is of sitting on a small brick wall. I was three, as was my sister, Sarah, who sat next to me. My dad stood in front of us.

We lived on the bottom floor of a two family house. It was small and contained, and stifling. We were balls of energy and we needed release; we needed to move.

My dad would take us all over the neighborhood, to different playgrounds. We played "Old Man," a variation of tag where my dad was always it. He would stand under the slide trying to grab our legs as we ran up and down. We shouted, "Old Man, you can't catch us," while sticking out our tongues, and shrieking in delight as he pretended to not be able to keep up.

We could do this for hours. Like playing fetch with a rambunctious puppy, my dad chased us until we were ready to drop. Then we'd go home and feel a little less stir-crazy on the bottom floor of that two-family house, an apartment and yard that never truly felt our own.

***

On the day of my first memory, Sarah and I got a second wind as we walked home from the park. We saw a small brick wall, separating someone's yard from the sidewalk. Though the wall would fall well below my hip today, at the time it felt like being on top of the world.

The wall was stepped, with three different levels. Sarah and I walked up the first one together, and then we both climbed to the second. She sat down and dangled her legs, her sneakers hanging half a foot from the ground. She was content with her medium-level ascent.

But, ever the daredevil, I wanted to go one step higher. I wanted to go all the way to the top.

So I climbed up and sat down. I was just far enough from Sarah to really test my dad's wingspan.

My sister and I were a tag team. We shared a room, our two little red iron beds were set up directly across from each other so when we opened our eyes in the morning we were each other's first sights. When my dad would try to put us down for naps, one of us would wait until he was trying to get the other to settle down, and then we would pop up and create a bigger disruption so he had to switch sides. The day we stopped being required to take naps was the day that Sarah drilled him in the head with her bottle from across the room as he tried to prevent my escape.

As we sat on this wall, on this sunny afternoon, we fed off each other's manic energies. We both began rocking forward, our tiny fists clasping onto the concrete ledge of the brick wall. My dad put his arms out in both directions, trying to create safety restraints for both of us.

As he kept us from falling, Sarah and I were progressively having more and more fun. We kept rocking our bodies harder and harder. Sarah went too hard first, and my dad lunged to keep her from hitting the ground.

Unfortunately, this coincided with my strongest jolt, as well, and as he attended to her, I let go of the wall mid-rock and allowed my body to be propelled straight forward.

My dad saw me begin my descent, but he could not make his way back over in time.

I smashed my head into the sidewalk and learned there is no one who can catch you every time you think it's safe to let go.

***

My memory of the day ends there, but the rest of the afternoon has been filled in for me. I cried for a bit after my head hit the ground, but I generally seemed okay, at first. My dad walked Sarah and me the few blocks back to our apartment.

At home, he became increasingly concerned. I was disoriented, my pupils were huge and my eyes were out of focus. When he spoke to me, I didn't seem to process what he was saying. He called my mom, who was at work. She drove home immediately. They left Sarah with a neighbor and drove me to the hospital.

***

At the hospital, the doctor diagnosed my concussion, and announced that I had to spend the night in the hospital. My mom left to go take care of Sarah, but my dad stayed with me; he felt guilty that he had not been able to protect me.

I remember staying up late that night watching TV. I had been throwing up and couldn't eat solid foods, so I was given an endless supply of popsicles, instead.

The next day, when I woke up, my mom brought me a plastic bullfrog to play with while I rested in a hospital bed. It was the kind of plastic frog whose mouth was open and a hard piece of plastic blocked off the wall to its cavernous interior. The piece of plastic was solid, unmoving, save for a small hole. The opening was like a pinprick through which you could squeeze hard and bring water into the frog's would-be stomach. Then you could squash it with your toddler might to spray water into the face of an unsuspecting victim.

I was concussed, and in a linoleum chamber instead of a pool; I had to entertain myself by holding the frog in front of my face. I repeatedly compressed the bullfrog, blowing hot gusts of polyvinyl scented air into my nostrils.

***

I remember being sad when the doctor came in and told me that it was okay for me to leave.

I wasn't afraid of the hospital; I liked it. There was something comforting about the constant ruckus in the halls; the carts being pushed and the reverberating chatter as nurses made their rounds.

I liked the TV, with the remote I controlled; I liked the seemingly endless supply of channels. But, most of all, there was something I liked about being sick, about being able to curl up into a little ball of vulnerability. It was like having a giant sleepover with my dad in a hotel, but in a place even more curious. I liked being brought gifts, and having people concerned about me, constantly asking me how I felt, how I was doing.

I liked people feeling sorry for me.

I didn't want to leave. I wanted to stay in the hospital forever.

***

When I was little I loved medicine. My parents kept Orange Triaminic in the condiment section of the fridge. Whenever the door opened, there it was, right at eye level.

That glowing bottle of citrus elixir called for me.

"I don't feel good," I would sniffle to my dad.

"Get some sleep," he would reply.

"Can I have some of the orange stuff?" I would ask, lightly coughing.

"Okay," he would say. "Go grab it."

I would walk to the fridge, fighting the urge to skip; I was giddy inside. This was my childhood version of picking your poison, though it was never much a decision, at all. I knew what I wanted. I had been thinking about it for hours.

He would pour some of the syrup onto a spoon and I would lap it down. It was like candy, but better.

Candy tasted good, but Triaminic felt good.

I took pleasure in knowing the stuff was moving through my body, fighting off any sickness.

Even if I knew I was not sick, per se, I figured there was nothing wrong with taking a little extra precaution.

***

When my parents bought us Flintstone Vitamins, I always wanted to take more than they gave me.

"You can't take more, or you'll get sick," my mom said.

But to my childhood mind, that seemed so counterintuitive.

How could medicine be bad for you? How could something that felt good be wrong? Shouldn't taking more of something just make it work better?

{ 4 }

Fear

When I was six or seven, I was consumed by obsessive thoughts that I was one day inevitably going to be kidnapped. I had vivid and disturbing dreams of being chased down by creepy men in rusty cars that slowly rolled down the street. The captor in the dream would vary; one night he would appear as Steve Martin, and the next night he might be Beetlejuice. No matter who the captor was, or how hard I would try to run away, I was never fast enough. He would always grab me to take me away from everyone I loved, forever.

Each night, as I went to bed, I would slowly look around and silently mouth goodbye to all of the items in my room, from stuffed animals to old family pictures. I shared a room with my little brother, who was four years younger than me. Most nights, my dad or mom would fall asleep in his bed. Our beds were pushed together, forming an L-shape in the corner of the room. As I fell asleep, I softly rested my hand against the back of whichever parent was in his bed.

So long as I fall asleep still touching them, this will not be the night I disappear, I told myself.

***

As my brother and his friends played hide and seek in our neighborhood, I would often sit on the porch and watch. Whenever he was "It" and had to count at the tree by himself, my stomach tensed with the fear that some car might come skidding down the street and take him away from us forever.

I would sit there, in the cold autumn air, wearing oversized athletic shorts and a gray fleece hoodie from the GAP. I was so anxious that I was almost numb. I would sit there on brisk afternoons, as my mother vacuumed in the living room beyond the screen door. I would sit there, extending my feet to reach into the splashes of sun that stretched across the green painted floorboards of the porch. I would sit there, paralyzed and transfixed by the fears that felt all too real. I would sit there, for hours, waiting for the worst to happen.

***

As I approached my tenth birthday, my family and I were driving back from Canada and decided to stop at Martin's Fantasy Island, an old amusement park near Niagara Falls. My sister I wanted to ride a roller coaster. She had just begun that 5th grade stage of puberty, where girls begin to gain weight and develop their first semblance of breasts.

As we loaded the crazy mouse, a middle-aged attendant with oily gray hair – and glasses that resembled those of the man who killed Susie Salmon – checked our lap bar. I watched as his eyes rested for a bit too long on my young sister's burgeoning chest. For the rest of the night, I was quiet as the image replayed itself in my head. We loaded into the van to drive away, and I lay in the back seat and puzzled over the way he had looked at my sister, a child.

Was our childhood over?

I pretended to sleep and silently cried.

{ 5 }

RX

Terry's office was like any other pediatricians, but with diagrams of faces displaying every emotion that one could even possibly imagine feeling covering the walls.

Terry played a crucial role in my childhood from sixth grade on, as I went on Zoloft then off of Zoloft; on Prozac then off of Prozac; on Lexapro and then off of Lexapro. Whatever medication she prescribed, I was always convinced she was on twice as high a dose.

Going to Terry felt punitive; I believed being on antidepressants meant there was something wrong with me; it felt like a secret I had to keep.

"Sometimes I feel depressed," I said to her.

"Let's get you an SSRI," she answered. "Or maybe you need a mood stabilizer like Welbutrin?"

Maybe I just need to feel, I thought.

But, I didn't say that.

Instead I accepted her diagnosis and agreed to try her prescription. The next morning, I always swallowed the pill.

{ 6 }

Unhappy

"Let's do prank calls."

I was feeling rather bored at a seventh grade sleepover birthday party, and I realized I would have to be the one to add some excitement.

"Okay," said the birthday boy as he left the room.

He came back a minute later carrying a phonebook. He pushed it in my direction, smirking.

"You first," he said.

"Fine," I replied, confidently.

I thumbed through the phonebook until I found the number for Taco Bell.

I dialed the number and waited for someone to answer.

"Taco Bell," the voice announced.

"Hello, sir," I chirped. "I just bought a cheesy bean and rice burrito, and I wanted to let you know that when I bit in, I found a finger inside."

"A what?"

"A finger," I started to giggle.

"Fuck off, kid. Get a life."

Click.

"Asshole," I said into the dial tone, proud of my new vocabulary.

"My turn," said the birthday boy, as he grabbed the phone and dialed the phone number to the local hip-hop station.

"Fire 106.7"

"I'd like to hear Barry Manilow, please."

"Who?"

"Barry Manilow."

Click.

He called again requesting Elton John, and then he called again requesting a Quaker hymn we were being made to sing in our middle school chorus.

He decided to stop calling after the person on the line said he'd call the police should he call again.

We went around the room, each person trying to upstage the person who had gone before.

It became my turn again, and I decided my time had come to take the cake.

I wanted to be funny, and I wanted to be the one who was unafraid.

So, I decided to prank call the mayor. I picked up the phone and dialed. When I got the voicemail of the mayor's office, I screeched into the phone with a bizarre Staten Island accent about some fictional school, "MY DAWTA TELLS ME THE GYM TEACHA GETS A LITTLE TOO CLOSE DURING WIFFLE BALL. IS THIS TRUE?"

The other boys were laughing, so I hung up, fearing they might be heard in the background.

A wave of anxiety washed over me, as I realized I had made a devastating mistake.

I'd forgotten to press *67, and, now I had a very strong feeling I was fucked.

***

As soon as I woke up I could tell something was wrong.

Almost immediately, the birthday boy's dad came into the room.

"The mayor just called," he said. "Apparently a 'frantic woman' left a message on his voicemail complaining about a gym teacher making her daughter uncomfortable."

He stared at me while he said this, and I knew I'd been caught. Someone had snitched.

"I'm calling all of your parents," he said. "Unless someone owns up to it."

"I did it," I begrudgingly said, furious that I should be the only one to get in trouble when everyone else had been along for the ride.

We all gathered our stuff and headed home. I was only a block away from my house, but that short distance felt like an eternity as I dragged my feet as slowly as possible. It was the dead of January, and the street was covered in ice. My feet made loud scraping sounds as I dug them into the earth, anxiously resisting my own steps toward home.

Fear outweighed defiance; much sooner than I would have liked, I arrived at my front door.

My mom and dad were waiting.

"Sit down," my dad said.

"It wasn't just me," I whined before even allowing them to begin lecturing. "We were all making prank calls."

"But you were the one who took it too far," my dad said.

"You don't even know what the other kids were saying!" I tried to argue. "They just didn't get caught!"

"No one else called the mayor," he said. "What were you thinking? You're smarter than this. This is humiliating for you and for us."

"I didn't think it was that big of a deal," I lied.

In actuality, I didn't think that I would get busted.

"You need to call the mayor and apologize," my dad said.

"When?" I whined.

"Give it a day," he said.

***

I went up to my room to sulk. I was going to lie down, when suddenly a strange idea crept into my head.

No, I thought. *No*

I kept trying to push this peculiar thought out of my head; I wanted the idea to go away. Yet, it was only becoming stronger.

I'd been reading *Riding in Cars with Boys*, and was fascinated by the scene where Beverly Donofrio describes slowly swallowing a bottle of pills.

I can do that too, I thought. *I can cry out for help, and no one will be mad at me because they'll know I'm hurting, too. They'll know I'm not just cruel and bad.*

I took a deep breath and looked at myself in the mirror. I locked my gaze upon the reflection of my own brown eyes.

I waited for my heart to palpitate; I expected tears to pour out as I apologized to myself for even thinking about inflicting self-harm.

I thought about the gravity of what could happen: I could get hurt; I could die.

I waited for myself to back out, but I didn't.

I felt apathetic.

Maybe I really can do this; maybe I will.

***

I crept down the stairs to the kitchen and poured Sprite into a glass. Walking over to the fridge, I reached up and grabbed a bottle of blue raspberry syrup. I poured the syrup into my cup and got a curly straw from the cupboard.

With my blue Shirley Temple in tow, I walked back up the stairs.

With each step, the idea became more real; I felt a strange wave of glee, and then an eerie calm.

This is a good solution, I thought. *It will make people understand how I feel.*

Once back in my room, I took my bottle of Zoloft off the dresser. As I removed each pill, one by one, I thought about what I was about to do. I didn't know what overdosing on Zoloft might do to my body. I was surprised at how little I cared.

I swallowed each pill individually, and took a sip of my mocktail to wash each down my throat.

The drink, and the straw felt so juvenile, while the action felt so adult.

After swallowing twenty pills, the thought suddenly struck that perhaps I wouldn't be able to come back from this. I suddenly remembered all the stories I'd ever heard of celebrities dying from drug overdoses. Images of Elvis on a toilet, and Marilyn Monroe in a coffin flashed into my mind.

I thought of Virginia Woolf at the bottom of a river, and Sylvia Plath in her kitchen full of gas.

I couldn't help but wonder if they had also gone into it not planning to go all the way.

I sprinted downstairs to the living room, where my mom and dad were sitting on a couch, ever unsuspecting.

"I just took twenty pills," I sobbed.

"What!" my mom shrieked. "Of what?"

"Zoloft," I babbled.

"Take him to the emergency room," my mom screamed to my dad.

My dad dragged me to the car.

On the ride to the hospital, I couldn't stop crying like a baby, and never stopped gripping my dad's arm.

Where I had just felt so rebellious moments before, I was now so aware of my age, of my youth.

I started to think of all that I might lose.

I was only 13.

***

At the hospital I lay in a bed in a little room by myself. One of the nurses happened to be the mother of one of my fifth grade classmates. I was bothered that she knew my secret.

A different nurse came in and handed me a Styrofoam cup full of liquid charcoal.

"Drink it all," she said, coldly.

It was gritty and jet-black, like wet tar. I chugged it and almost immediately spewed midnight-colored vomit all over the white linoleum floors.

"Is that supposed to happen?" my dad asked when the nurse walked in and saw the mess splattered across the room.

She drew a tight breath.

"That's one way to get it out."

***

Scoop. Drop. Drop. Drop. Scoop. Drop. Drop. Eye contact. Silence.

My therapist, Lisa, and I were attempting to amend our relationship. To say that we had started off on the wrong foot would be beyond an understatement. During sessions with my whole family, no matter what the initial topic, the discussion would end with me furiously yelling at Lisa after her questionably intentional provocation.

As a result, I'd refused to go back to her.

Now, because of the pill incident, I found myself in Lisa's office playing Mancala.

I had already convinced the nurses, doctors, psychiatrists and my parents that my mass swallowing of pills was not an actual suicide attempt, but rather a cry for help.

That reality is easiest for everyone, I thought. Though I am not quite so sure anymore what is true and what is false.

"So why did you do it?" she asked.

The truth was that I really did not know how to verbalize the turmoil within my body, the shaking within my soul. I was not completely miserable, and I didn't actually want to be dead, I now realized.

The thought of people thinking I was suicidal made me quite uncomfortable. While other kids in my class had begun wearing all black and cutting their wrists, purposefully allowing their wounds to show, I wore Abercrombie and ran cross-country.

But, secretly I knew, we were not so different.

Part of me was jealous of their ability to outwardly cry for help; to announce they were not okay.

I was much too interested in mainstream acceptance to be so outward. I tried to keep my suffering to myself.

Yet, something inside of me was off. When little things went wrong, I had extreme reactions. I threw things; I burst into tears. I was so sensitive.

"Do you think you're unhappy with something about yourself?" she asked.

This was not a question I was unfamiliar with. Whenever I seemed to get upset with anyone I always waited for this question – from my parents, teachers, aunts.

Just ask the question already, I thought. *Just ask me if I am gay.*

And weirdly, unlike most people who strayed away from the question, she asked.

"Do you think you're gay?"

"Yes," I responded, marking the first time I had ever said it aloud.

"When did you realize?" she asked.

Silence.

"Do you not want to talk about it?"

"Nope," I responded.

So it was done: The question had been asked, the answer given.

I had verbalized why I was so unhappy. But, that didn't make me feel any better.

I had given life to my greatest fear: Having said it aloud, I knew I was truly gay; it would never go away.

I was a gay 13-year-old in a place that was neither especially progressive nor oppressive.

I was so scared to embody my sexuality.

I didn't want to pretend to like girls, so I decided I wouldn't.

I just wouldn't talk about it all.

And so it would be, for the next few years, until I could run off to New York or Paris, some city where I could get lost in the liberal fabric, that I would handle this topic in the same way that I handled the pauses between the scoops and drops of Mancala turns with Lisa; I would handle it with silence.

{ 7 }

Coming Out

"When did you come out?" I am often asked by friends – mostly who are straight. How do you even begin to answer that? Coming out isn't a moment, it's a process; it's freeing and it's painful.

Coming out isn't always an act of self-liberation or a statement of pride. I came out to my parents during my freshmen year of high school because I'd gotten in trouble and I wanted them to feel bad for me; I came out to a boy or two moments after they came out to me; I came out to some friends as a teen by accident when too many cans of Keystone Light made my lips much looser; and I came out to some friends only once at college, where the free-spirited atmosphere made me finally feel home in my own skin.

To me, the most crucial moment was when I came out to myself.

* * *

I was home alone in 6th grade, watching TV in my parent's bed. It was a hot summer day, and I wore my usual uniform of an oversized t-shirt and basketball shorts. My cheeks were still puffy and full like a child and baby fat still clung to my hips, but the sprouting of hair in the most peculiar of places made me aware that a bodily transition was underway.

Yet, no prepubescent child can fully comprehend the emotional, physical, and spiritual changes that accompany sexual development. No almost adolescent can ever be prepared for the way this transformation hits like a tsunami. No matter how many sex-ed classes you sit through, no matter how many mini-deodorants you are given, no matter how many illustrations you stare at in "It's Perfectly Normal," no matter how many condoms you put on bananas, you can't ever understand any of it, until it actually happens to you.

How can you be warned that you will spend the next decade held hostage by the surge of the onset of your sexuality; how, like a sailor lost at sea, you'll be violently flipped while your exposed skin is ground into the gritty sand as you're pulled out into the rough wake? And there's no respite; you'll feel equally out of control as you're thrown back to shore, only to immediately be washed back out; your bodily reactions, your feelings, they're all so out of your control. And there's no one to properly tell you to grab a life vest and hold on, because by the time they're old enough to warn you, they've forgotten how it feels; how rousing and terrifying it is to not understand not only what's happening below your belt, but also in your mind; in your conscious thoughts and in your fantasies.

So I sat on the bed, ever unsuspecting, watching an infomercial; what could be more innocuous? A man and a woman were demonstrating their fitness regiment on some bullshit abs machine that YOU TOO COULD FOREVER TRANSFORM YOUR BODY WITH FOR JUST THREE PAYMENTS OF $39.99 PLUS SHIPPING AND HANDLING.

The woman wore a lime green sports bra and tight lycra cycling shorts, the man was shirtless, wearing just black workout shorts. Both of their bodies looked as though Michelangelo had sculpted them, and as they went through the tediously dull workout, sweat glistened on their bare torsos.

Every child knows that infomercials are a sign from God to find a new channel, and I was sitting in bed eating ice cream; I didn't give two shits about working out. But, I found myself transfixed by what was happening on the screen.

I was disturbed and perplexed by own fascination, by my involuntarily held gaze.

What am I looking at?

I paid attention to my own eyes' desire, and realized that I was focused on one thing: the man's exposed body.

I felt a stirring below, and realized my body was reacting to what my eyes were seeing. I felt my face grow flushed as desire filled my veins; a desire I had never experienced before. Of course every young boy has involuntary erections, but this was my first that was inspired by sexual attraction; my first arousal, the first time blood had been called to my groin by lust.

Shit, I thought. I'm gay.

* * *

Having a sexual awakening is hard for anyone, but it is so much worse when you are fighting against yourself; when you are not just confused by your desires, but rather repulsed by them.

I don't want to be gay, I told myself. Maybe this is just a phase.

It didn't take me long to realize that my sexuality was not temporary; my fantasies were always male-dominated.

Of course, this shouldn't have come as much of a surprise; I'd been called gay many times before as a child. But, those names were attached to effeminate mannerisms and qualities and an interest in objects and subjects that were boxed-off as being "for girls."

This was different. Now, my body was physically declaring its sexuality, its homosexuality. I was without a choice. And that was terrifying.

Plus, there'd been some evidence that had been confusing; subconscious manifestations of my own denial, of my own fear. When I was five, my best friend – who was a girl – and I had a fake wedding; we'd skinny dipped in her pool, French kissed in my closet and had played countless rounds of "I'll show you mine if you show me yours."

In elementary school, I'd had crushes on girls, and many of them felt real. When I played The Sims with my guy friends, we'd create replicas of ourselves with wives who were just grown up versions of girls from our class.

And now, here I was, in middle school, with a scary truth that I had to guard to protect myself.

I had to keep this a secret.

* * *

Of course, it was glaringly obvious, but I still went through the protocol.

Mind your eyes in the locker room, don't be that gay who creeps on straight boys, keep publicly having "crushes" on girls and, most importantly, never allow yourself to be subjugated; establish social dominance and power and intimidate so you'll never be a victim.

The first two rules weren't so hard to maintain. I had one fleeting faux-relationship in 6th grade with a serial dating, lonely 8th grade girl and then decided that faking it wasn't really my thing. So I maintained public asexuality, and rather put all of my energy into the third rule:

If people are afraid of me, they won't probe. So I suppose I'd rather be feared than loved.

* * *

The morning when I was 22 and called my dad sobbing to tell him I was an alcoholic, I remember admitting, "I just feel so mean."

"When you were young, you hardened yourself. You became a prick, so no one could hurt you," he said. "But sometimes you've got to let yourself just be soft."

That is something I am still working on, but while growing up, that was the least of my concerns.

In middle school culture, where "faggot" is a common phrase, used both as a homophobic slur and a synonym of "asshole," and "that's so gay" is a term stated to describe pretty much anything negative; I couldn't help but internalize feelings of self-loathing. When people would direct such terms at me, or even imply them, I would use physical and social dominance to intimidate; I "put them in their place" because I believed it was a dog-eat-dog world and I didn't want to be put into mine.

Of course, in retrospect, there are many instances in middle and high school where I now realize I went too far in what I thought was self-protection; I became the bully to avoid being the bullied. It troubles me that when I was in the moment, and I felt threatened, it was so hard to discern between self-preservation and cruelty.

In hostile environments, I can't help but become hostile, I convinced myself.

* * *

This trend continued through high school, where I was never particularly kind or empathetic to other gay students who were 'out' because they reminded me too much of a part of myself that I wanted to hide. When I got to college and saw cliques of gay men form – full of people who I deemed "radical" in their ability to not only embrace but also actively assert their queerness – I quickly decided that these were people I wanted to avoid.

I didn't want to go to gay bars and be shirtless and sexual, I wanted a town house and a husband who wears loafers while pushing our double stroller and walking our dog.

I wanted to conform to the existing heteronormative lifestyle; I wanted to find my future husband who was equally keen to be sectioned off from the greater LGBTQ community so we could more easily blend into the straight world. I had spent so many years working so hard to fit in; laboring to create my little corner of space.

But, life's not that simple, and vilifying an identity group you belong to so you can be a token minority in the hegemonic group is never going to make you happy; it's always going to come back to bite you; it will make you forever hate yourself.

And that lesson I learned, as I let down my walls and made gay friends; I learned it as I realized I could have gay friends who I did not sleep with – who I was not only friends with because I thought they could one day be cast in the role of "picture perfect husband." I learned this lesson as I realized that I do in fact care about gay rights, not only because fighting for LGBTQ equality was tied to the end of my own oppression, but more importantly because – apart from my sexuality – I am in so many ways privileged.

And so, though I once so subconsciously daydreamed about finding my husband and running away to blend into "mainstream" America, that mentality was so beyond fucked up; it was motivated by the selfishness that stemmed from my raging self-loathing.

* * *

On National Coming Out Day, my newsfeed fills with Rainbow Flags posted by those who are proud and declarative of their sexuality and those who are proud and declarative of the sexuality of their loved ones: laws have been written that guarantee my right to marry – a right that as I grew up I was unsure I would ever have, a right that so many were denied: videos go viral that assure suffering LGBTQ youth that "It Gets Better." Yet, I cannot help but hope that one day such holidays and campaigns become obsolete: I can't help but hope that "coming out" stops being terrifying and earth-shattering, that parents won't be angry when their kids come out because they're assholes or sad that their kids come out because "it's difficult to know that life will always be harder for them," that trans-women of color stop being assaulted and murdered and that no kids – or adults for that matter – need to hear that "It Gets Better" because we will be at a point where "It is Better," not just on October 11th, but all year round.

{ 8 }

Firsts

"You grab one too," I whispered to my friend as I reached into the cooler full of melting ice and fished out a cold bottle of beer, immediately shoving it up my shirt.

My friend pulled one out too, and we ran off into his backyard where two of our other friends were already waiting.

After taking the top off the bottles with a keychain, we took turns gulping down the fizzing amber liquid. The beer tasted like shit, but I was instantly enamored with the warm feeling rushing through my body; I loved the light buzz that happened in my head just a few moments after the beer hit my stomach.

Quickly, we finished the two beers.

"I think I'm drunk," I said, so proud of myself.

"Me too," agreed my friend; his face looked unconvinced.

We walked around the yard with the same cautious curiosity an astronaut might have on their first time exploring the gravity-deprived moon. We started doing things we would normally do – swinging on a swing, climbing a tree – but in slow motion; we moved through the world, trying to feel how we thought being drunk *should* feel.

"Wow, I bet I'm so much better at basketball when I drink," I said as I picked up a resting ball and hurled it overhand toward a hoop, completely missing.

"I can barely walk a straight line!" said my friend, as he giggled and slumped toward the ground theatrically after taking one baby step.

***

Of course, even more exciting than actually consuming alcohol, was getting to tell everyone at school on Monday that we were now officially drinkers.

"Yeah, it was pretty crazy," I told the rest of our friends at lunch. "But, it sucked to wake up hungover."

Of course, being in eighth grade, my friends and I were still too young to go to the field parties that took place in the woods behind the power plant and near the water tower at the neighborhood reservoir.

But, against our parents' wishes, we all had Facebook accounts. I would spend hours clicking through the pictures of the older kids I knew chugging Smirnoff Ice and Bud Light around a bonfire.

Soon I'll be there too, I told myself.

I, for one, felt certain that there wasn't some invisible line we would cross as we switched over from the middle school to the high school that next summer.

"Now is just as a good a time as any to start drinking...really drinking," I told my friends. "This way, we'll know how to hold our liquor by the time we actually are allowed to go to the high school parties."

So, we started drinking whenever we could. After our cross-country meets on Saturday mornings, we would rush to the house of whoever's parents were least likely to be home. After carefully surveying the area, we would throw open the doors of liquor cabinets and greedily grab bottles.

We would sip from the bottles, until we eventually graduated to taking full shots.

Everything is more fun after drinking, I thought. So I started drinking before everything I possibly could. I took a chug before going to the movies, and a gulp before the Friday night football games.

My dad was in early recovery, so there usually wasn't much alcohol in my house. Plus, my mom and dad were almost always home. Needless to say, I quickly decided to never use my house as the hangout spot.

We invented our first mixed drink, which we called Jamaica Um? The drink was a late middle school staple, as it had no set recipe and was made by pouring a little bit of alcohol from each bottle into a glass.

A splash of blue curacao; a pour of tequila; a shot of vodka.

Once the contents had been properly swirled together, we took turns chugging the mixture that smelled like paint thinner and felt like Hydrochloric acid as it slid down our throats.

We were careful to watch which alcohol the adults drank the most, as that was the one they would be least likely to notice missing when we later dipped into the bottle. We figured that as the contents kept gradually sinking lower, the parents at hand would just assume that they themselves had consumed the liquor.

***

An hour before my eighth grade band concert, I went off with my sister and her friends to try smoking weed. We walked down a path through a thicket and settled in a small clearing that overlooked the driveway of the high school I would be entering the next year.

We sat cross-legged in a circle, and my sister's friend took out her bowl, screens and a small plastic baggy half-filled with weed. I watched her put the screen into the bowl's reservoir, and then pack the weed on top of it. She lit the bowl from above, and then she inhaled deeply. A moment of silence, then there was a crackling sound like a child blowing bubbles into their milk through a straw.

I didn't let my eyes drift away.

I want to know how to do it; I want to smoke the bowl right.

They passed the bowl around, and I watched each person deeply inhale the thick smoke after skillfully lighting the small pile of weed without burning their fingertips.

Then, it was my turn.

"Cover the carb, and just pull it back deep," the resident pothead said as I lifted the bowl toward my mouth. "Swirl it around then let it out."

I did as I was told.

"Yeah! There you go."

We kept passing the bowl in a circle.

I took more hits; the more I smoked the less I felt like speaking.

Everyone else was chatty and giggling, but I just felt anxious. My ability to communicate was shrinking, as I pulled deeper into my mind.

Perhaps this isn't the drug for me.

***

Everything felt like it was moving slowly.

I wanted to skip the band concert and go home and get into my bed, but knew I couldn't. I fake played my trombone as I struggled to focus on anything besides the waves of panic washing through my mind.

It felt as though everyone was watching me. Of course they partially were, as I was on a stage playing an instrument. Yet, my high paranoia made me only able to focus on myself: I forgot they were not looking at *me the person* but rather at *us the band*.

I went through the motions of playing the instrument, and hoping no one could hear the absence of my sound.

In the back of my head, I couldn't help but keep thinking about how we were playing on the same stage where only two years earlier I'd been picked as the class representative to deliver an anti-drug speech at an assembly.

I was so certain I'd never do drugs.

I couldn't decide whether I wanted to laugh or cry at this thought; my emotional disorientation must have been highly readable on my face.

"How high are you?" my friend whispered. "Your eyes look so weird."

"Soooo high," I whispered back, proud of my defiance, yet highly aware of the hollow sound of my own voice.

"Do you like how it feels?" the friend asked.

"I love it," I lied. "It feels so cool."

***

On a Friday night during the summer after eighth grade, I sat watching TV with my friend in his basement.

I couldn't help but feel lame as I thought of the exciting plans older kids must have had; plans in which we were not included as 14-year-olds.

"Let's drink," I suggested.

"I don't feel like it," my friend responded. "But, you can."

Why would he choose not to drink?

I went up the stairs into the kitchen, where I poured whiskey into a glass and knocked it back. I refilled the glass with ginger ale, and went to pour more whiskey in, but my friend stopped me.

"We can't take anymore," he said. "My mom is going to notice soon."

"Just put some water in it," I said flippantly as I grabbed a bottle of nail polish on the counter. I unscrewed the top and started sniffing. "I heard this gets you high too."

"Seriously?"

"Wait," I responded, huffing deeper. I felt the fumes fill my throat and nasal passages. "It's working."

"Let me try," my friend said as he snatched the bottle from my hand.

{ 9 }

Puberty

It was the middle of the night when I woke up and walked to the bathroom. I took off my clothes off and threw them into a pile on the tiled floor. Staring at myself in the mirror, I was dissatisfied with what I saw.

I wished my hips were smaller, that my stomach was flatter, that my pecs were more developed.

Then I look at my lower pelvis, where the hair had now thickly grown in. Sometimes when I took a bath, I covered this area with a washcloth; it scared me.

I thought back to sixth grade, when hair had first grown under my arms. I remembered how I'd lifted my arms and stared into the mirror; how I'd ripped the hair out each night until there was none left.

I tried to picture the exact moment when I'd realized I'd lost that fight.

I could not put my finger on it.

Taking a razor from the cabinet, I dug the blade into the thick skin a few inches below my belly button, just above the hair.

I pulled the razor straight across, just hard enough to draw a light flow of blood. The blood poured down toward my developing manhood.

What I wanted, I was not sure: There was no way to stop time; I couldn't go backwards.

I took a shower and waited for the blood to stop flowing.

Then I went to bed.

{ 10 }

Escalation

One morning, before school, I was alone in the kitchen getting ready for the day. It was a morning just like any other, but I couldn't take my eyes off the box of wine that was nestled between the fridge and the oven.

Alcohol in our house was so rare. I knew the contents of a box of wine were so challenging for parents to monitor.

I'd hit a jackpot.

I suppose, I could have a glass, just one more time, I thought to myself.

Just the day before, I'd had a glass of wine with breakfast. Frankly, just that one glass had made the first few hours of high school feel all the more tolerable.

I poured myself a glass. The wine was chardonnay, and its yellow color was deep. The morning sun backlit the glass, and the richness of the color made it look as viscous as olive oil.

I chugged the first glass. I hadn't yet eaten breakfast, and almost immediately I felt the warmth in my stomach that spread like a welcomed fire through my veins.

One more glass can't hurt.

As soon as I indulged that thought, almost automatically, I poured myself another glass. This time, I filled it even closer to the brim.

I slurped it down.

I felt even better; I was so happy and giddy; I was elated; I felt so alive.

More, I thought. *How much more can I have without getting caught?*

I'd never before actually gotten drunk off of wine; I wasn't quite certain how big a glass of wine really was, or how much each glass would affect me.

I couldn't stumble my way through the hallways of school, so I figured I should stop after this glass.

I put the box down, and turned to walk away.

Something in me snapped; a shock of electricity ran from the top of my skull down my neck and back up.

I feel good, and I want to feel even better; I've had some, but I want even more.

Suddenly, I was ripping apart the cupboards. I was desperately searching for anything that I could use to transport wine to school.

I found an old see-through sippy cup and pulled it out. Bolting around the kitchen I was trying to get everything in order; I only had fifteen minutes to get to school.

I filled the cup to the top, and I took a huge swig. I then filled it to the top again.

Once having ensured it was closed tight; I threw the bottle in my backpack before sprinting out the door.

I departed so quickly that I didn't notice I'd left my lunch – in a small brown paper bag – sitting alone on the kitchen counter.

***

I drank through biology class, and then I walked to lunch.

By this time, news has spread among my classmates that not only was I drinking in school, but that I was blatantly drunk.

When my words begin lightly slurring during lunch, people laughed.

They're not laughing at me, I told myself. *They're laughing with me.*

They must appreciate my defiance; at least, that's what I convinced myself.

I walked into history after lunch, with my head fully buzzing, and my motor skills beginning to feel noticeably impaired. Everything felt fuzzy and bright.

The excitement had worn off, and now I wished I could just make my intoxication go away.

"Okay, guys, sit down and put all of your stuff away," the teacher said.

Shit, I remembered. *The test is today.*

I almost wanted to laugh, but I held it in.

That would be so obvious.

Discretely, I shoved a piece a gum into my mouth as the teacher made her way toward my desk.

"Thank you," I said, noticing that my voice sounded strange and sloppy, not quite my own.

She began to furrow her brow, but I was strangely ready: I coughed, acting as though I had something stuck in my throat.

A beat passed, and someone called her name.

She moved on.

***

A week before my fifteenth Christmas, I heavily drank whiskey with my friend.

We took shot after shot; we pounded them, as we had never done before.

Our energy levels rose and rose, until I was certain I was about to burst.

"Let's go sledding," I said.

"Okay," he agreed.

As we ran around our neighborhood, the recent dusting of snow covered every imaginable surface, making it look like a Christmas village. The weather was frigid, but the alcohol was keeping us warm.

Getting this drunk made the whole world feel like a playground; it was like being transported to an alternate reality. This feeling was so refreshing, and all I could think about was how much I wanted more alcohol.

How can I get it?

I texted a girl in our class who I knew liked to drink. She had parents who were happy to look the other way, when they were even home.

"Are you home?" I asked.

She was.

Perfect.

We stopped at her house, not far from my own. After quickly exchanging pleasantries. I cut to the chase.

"Let's drink."

"Okay," she said.

We bee lined it for her parent's liquor cabinet.

I grabbed a bottle of cognac that was covered in dust. It looked unloved; it looked like liquor that wouldn't be missed.

I took a swig from the bottle and then passed it off to my friend.

He put it down.

"Drink some!" I exclaimed.

"I'm already drunk," he replied.

"Fine," I conceded. "Then I'll just take your share."

I took another gulp, and immediately burped. Fire rose in my throat, as my stomach tried to reject the cognac. I was scared I might throw up, as saliva filled my mouth. I kept swallowing the saliva, and breathing through my nose until, finally my stomach settled.

"Let's go sledding," I shouted, marching toward the door.

***

At the reservoir, we climbed to the top of the water tower hill. From the top of the hill, you could see for miles; the streetlights of Syracuse sparkled like a fallen night's sky. This was the spot teenagers had been drinking for generations; it was finally our turn to begin this rite of passage.

In this state, we could have been trekking to the summit of Everest. Through drunken eyes, the whole world felt new and exciting.

At the top of the hill, we immediately ran into a group of upper-classmen girls who were 'sledding' too.

They were the cool girls from our high school; the girls who threw parties at their parents' houses, had sex with whomever they wanted and did coke. They didn't care about school, or expectations; they just did what they pleased.

As a type-A person at heart, I was envious of their seeming aversion to judgment and expectations. I desperately sought their approval.

They welcomed us into their circle of inflated snow tubs. They were all sprawled on the icy ground, bundled up in their snow pants, mittens and gloves. We must have looked like children from afar; this is what we all did when we were little.

Of course, now, there was one big difference: Intoxication.

The ringleader pulled out a bottle of apple-flavored rum. After taking a swig, she passed it to me.

I took a sip.

It tasted so sweet, just like candy.

Compared to the harshness of the alcohol from earlier, this stuff barely even had a burn.

I chugged from the bottle. The more I drank, the less I tasted. What once would have made me gag now went down as though it was water.

We took turns drinking straight from the bottle. After a few rounds, I felt so drunk that I needed to lie down.

I draped myself across the ringleader's lap, and remembered how freezing the air had felt as it touched my face earlier. Now, I couldn't feel much anything; my face was numb, but none of it felt scary; it was strangely comforting.

The icy winds whipping across my flushed face reminded me of jumping into a lake on a hot summer day.

"I'm so drunk," I tried to whisper to the girl on whom I lied, but my words just came out as gibberish. I barely could understand myself, and I actually knew what I was trying to say.

"What are you saying?" she laughed.

I opened my mouth to tell her again, but then I decided that it didn't really matter.

I rolled off of her and put my face down into the hard frozen snow.

***

When I came to I was being dragged down the front steps of a house. I tried to walk down a step but I stumbled.

I fell straight into the arms of a man; I could feel his body buckle under the force of my weight. He somehow managed to stay standing.

"Seamus!" the man shouted. "Seamus, wake up and talk to us."

"Dad?" I grumbled, barely able to open my mouth.

I had never been this blacked out; this incapacitated. I came in and out of consciousness. One moment, I could hear, and then the next I couldn't.

I was there, and then I was gone.

Whenever I came to, I tried to answer the last question I could remember being asked.

Mumbling out any answer, let alone a coherent one, took a great deal of energy and strength; I was lacking both.

"I fell and hit my head on a rock," I managed to slur; foolishly hoping they might not realize I was drunk.

"He hit his head?" my mom shrieked.

"No, he didn't," said a woman who had just appeared from no-where. "He's just had too much to drink. Just get him to bed."

"We're taking him to the hospital," shouted my dad.

***

Beep. Beep.

I woke up to a blinding fluorescent light.

Where am I?

I knew I wasn't in my bed, or even at my house, at all. As my eyes struggled to fully open, I realized I wasn't wearing any clothes; I was completely naked save for a piece of fabric that felt like a sheet draped over me.

Am I in a morgue?

My hands explored my body. A heart monitor was hooked up to my chest; through six sticky circles it clung to my skin.

I moved my hand lower and I felt a tube near my groin. I followed the tube and was startled to realize I had a catheter jammed up my urethra.

I tried to sit up.

I couldn't; I immediately collapsed. Never before had I felt such debilitating nausea. My body felt broken.

The nausea quickly grew in strength. I turned my head, convinced I was about to throw up on the floor.

Nothing came up. I dry heaved, but my stomach was completely empty.

When I finally gave up on pushing any toxins out my body, I lifted my head and saw my mom and dad. They were sitting in chairs against the wall; they were watching me.

An alarm went off in my head: I had gone way too far.

What have I done?

"Do you know where you are?" my mom asked.

I opened my mouth to speak, but my throat was so dry that nothing much came out.

I took a deep breath, and I tried again.

"The hospital" I croaked, immediately bursting into tears.

"What happened?"

"I don't know."

"Tell us who you were drinking with at the reservoir," my dad demanded, his voice breaking from fear.

Even in this state, where I was still wildly intoxicated, I knew better than to snitch. I knew exactly what would happen: My mom and dad would call some parents who would have no follow through, as they couldn't care less about what their children were doing out of sight.

Even still, the kids would get mad at me for drawing attention to their behavior.

I'm the one who will socially suffer if I tell the truth, I thought.

I was feeling quite sorry for myself, so I didn't tell them who I had been with. I decided that I wouldn't disclose much anything, at all.

"You have alcohol poisoning and hypothermia," my dad said, as his voice grew louder. "Your blood alcohol content was so high that your brain could have shut down."

"You could have died," my mom added, choking up. "You almost died. If you hadn't been with people, you would have lain in the snow and never gotten up."

"And you think you have the right to not tell us who you were with?" my dad seethed; he must have been so disgusted by my priorities.

My decision had been made. I didn't give them what they wanted; I didn't tell them who provided me with the surplus of alcohol, or who allowed me to get to that point of intoxication.

It was heartbreaking to watch. My mom and dad needed a villain to blame, because right at that moment the only villain they could see was me. They had seen me in hospital beds before, and they didn't want to think I was the one who did this to myself. That type of recklessness is a hard pill for parents to swallow.

I saw a different villain in the situation: Bad luck.

"It was just a freak accident," I said through tears.

"Accidents are coming home obviously drunk," my dad said. "Not almost killing yourself."

{ 11 }

Counsel

"Do you think you have a drinking problem?" asked my new alcohol counselor Meryl.

"Not really," I said, shifting in my seat and looking off.

"Then why did you get so drunk?"

"Because, I'm depressed," I said. By this point, I'd had a whole day to think out my responses.

"So you think if you weren't depressed you would be able to control your drinking?" she asked.

"Yes," I said.

"I want to be honest with you," she said. "I've heard that many times before. Almost always it isn't true."

Well, I thought. *They were wrong, but I am right.*

"Okay," I said, a hint of attitude emerging.

"Do you want to stop drinking?"

"No," I said, again averting my gaze off to the side.

"Do you think you should stop drinking?"

"For a little, I guess," I said half-heartedly.

"Usually the people I work with need to stop drinking," she said.

"Oh," I said; I started thinking about what I could say to ensure I would never need to come back. Though I knew I should at least pretend I didn't want to drink, I couldn't bring myself to do so; I wanted to defend what I saw as being my right to intoxication.

"Are you only here because your parents are making you come?"

"Yes," I said.

"Well," she said, slightly sighing. "Let's see what we can do."

{ 12 }

Loss

When I was 15, I reclined beneath a boy whom I did not particularly care about in the backseat of his car in a shadowy parking lot.

"Are you ready?" he asked, as he spit into his open palm and rubbed the saliva onto his manhood.

Though I was not dying to do this, I felt that it had reached the point where it would take more effort to decline.

"Yes," I said, as I let him spread my legs and I angled myself to be entered. He spit again, using it this time to lubricate the other logical location.

"Okay," he said, a bit too excited. "I'm going to push in, now."

I focused on a rip in the ceiling of his car, and kept my mouth far away from his, sealed shut.

"Oh!" I exclaimed, as I near convulsed from the pain that shot through my body. He began to lightly thrust, and it felt like I was being stabbed a million times, over and over again; it felt like the grotesquely reverse motion of King Arthur pulling the sword from the stone.

For a minute and a half, I shallowly breathed in and out through my nose as I cursed the gods for letting my path cross with the boy who now hovered above me.

"I'm going to finish," he panted, like a dehydrated dog.

He kept his word and soon it was over. The air in the car felt heavy, and the smell of completion had wafted to all corners of our nest, from the steering wheel to the rear windshield.

That was it? That was my first time? I thought to myself, rather disappointed, if not disturbed.

"How was it?" he asked, self-satisfied.

I felt filthy, but I feigned a smile.

"Good," I lied as I pulled my underwear back on and tried to find my shirt in the pile of carelessly strewn clothes on the floor. "Can you take me home?"

{ 13 }

Thin

When I was 11-years-old, I got stuck between two tires in a tunnel on playground.

My friend's mom had brought us, and when she could not pull me out, she enlisted the help of strong-looking men who were there with their own children. They grabbed me under my armpits and yanked as hard as they could.

"Suck in your stomach," they told me, but no matter how much I tried to deflate my body, I would not budge.

Someone called 911, and I was rescued when firefighters used the Jaws of Life to pry the two tires apart.

I emerged humiliated.

I'm fat. I'm fat. I'm fat.

I couldn't make the words stop screaming in my head.

That moment shaped how I viewed my body; my flesh felt so out of my control; I had told it to move and it didn't. The time I spent between the tires taught me that I existed as two entities, my mind and my body. The latter was defiant.

As the next few years of pre- and mid-pubescence rolled along, I was often reminded of how much I hated my body. Sure there was the tire incident, but there was also the moment when I realized I needed to buy husky jeans; the time when a 'friend' pointed out my 'big belly;' when I grew hair in my armpits before my friends.

I wore t-shirts when swimming and best attempted to hide the outline of my physical expanse beneath baggy clothing. Yet, I could never escape my feelings of self-disgust. Regardless of what covered me, I knew what lay underneath: Fat, imperfection and inconvenient bulk.

As eighth grade neared it's end, and high school, varsity cross country and the prospect of being a sexual being drew closer, I decided this was my moment to shed my baby fat; it was my time to become thin.

I began training for a ten-mile road race with my dad. We went running every night. Two-mile runs turned into five-mile runs, which eventually turned into ten-mile runs. The weight that I had always been ashamed of melted off my frame.

As I began my freshman year, I went from being a mediocre runner to one of the best on my team. I began being flooded with compliments about not only my appearance, but also my newfound athletic ability.

But, as I achieved 'healthiness,' I didn't want to stop there. I sped right on past.

I already didn't eat red meat, and I decided to give up poultry and seafood, as well. I traded in white bread for whole wheat, and 2% milk for skim. At first, almost subconsciously, my portions of food began shrinking. And so did I.

Like many things in life, drastic weight loss is a slippery slope. Like many other stories I have heard, my newfound passion for health very quickly took a sinister turn.

I started going for runs by myself after cross country, and when I heard John Tesh say something on the radio about weight loss happening when you made sure you ate at least two grams of fiber for every 90 calories, I didn't take that as a suggestion, it became my rule.

I often walked to the grocery store for fun, where I wandered the aisles trying to find new low and zero calorie products. From sugar free ice cream with fiber, to laxative chocolate, it wasn't hard in a-

binge-and-fast-obsessed-America to find foods and supplements that would aid my now full-fledged eating disorder.

I began having days where I only ate vegetables, which turned into days where I ate nothing at all. Eventually my body would crave food, but because of the deprivation, when I would finally eat, I would gorge. I would hide in my room and eat tubs of cookie dough and bag after bag of chips.

When I was done, I would lock myself in the bathroom where I chugged liters of water. Maniacal yet methodical, I always turned on the shower and the radio to hide the sounds of hacking as I rammed two fingers down my throat and vomited over and over until I thought I'd gotten it all out. When I'd look into the mirror, my eyes were glassy and bloodshot, but my seasonal allergies always provided the perfect excuse.

It didn't take long for 'You look great,' to change into commentary about exposed ribs and sunken eyes. When people expressed concern, I took it as a compliment.

Like any addiction, my eating disorder made me behave strangely; I retreated into myself and felt always alone. When I ate too much in public, I made excuses to go home so I could remove the sustenance from my body. When I went to meals with friends, I lied and said I'd already eaten and watched enviously as they ate 'normal' food without thinking twice.

One day while out at lunch with my mom, I made myself throw up in the restaurant bathroom. "Did you just throw up?" she asked when I sat back down. "No," I snapped angrily, making the subject change, even though all I really wanted was someone to make me stop.

Around this time, I began drinking heavily. Minimal eating and heavy drinking not so shockingly proved to be a dangerous combination. That fall just after turning 16, I spent a month in inpatient rehab after being hospitalized twice for alcohol poisoning.

In rehab, I quickly realized that most of my counselors were not interested in talking about my issues with eating. During my initial consultation, I'd decided to be honest about my habits, and when asked if I restricted eating or made myself throw up, I said yes to both. That was the last I heard about either topic during my thirty-day stay.

Though the counselors spent an hour going through my bag to make sure I didn't have hand sanitizer, no one ever thought to monitor whether I was just having an apple for lunch or skipping dinner altogether.

With alcohol and drugs taken away, I had all the more energy to invest in self-deprivation. So I did. What would it feel like to not have a problem? How would I deal with life without exercising this control?

I left rehab no less sick than I had been when I'd gone in, and I spent the next six years with all of the same habits. It always began with phases of restrictive eating, which were almost always followed by utterly out of control periods of binging and purging.

***

I recently logged into a secret Live Journal account I had kept as a 16-year-old. The settings were private, so only I could see what I wrote. What I found was disturbing.

In May of 2006, a little after midnight, I wrote a post that I titled 'New Diet:'

> *"Dearest Journal,*
> *I have just thought up my new amazing diet.*
> *Each day I will allow myself six (6) cans of any given 105 calorie-a-can, canned vegetables. Each can must be eaten an hour apart from each other. I will also be allowed one (1) bag of Healthy Choice popcorn. All beverages MUST be calorie free. Drink as much green tea as possible. If any food is eaten outside of the vegetables OR popcorn it MUST BE VOMITED. Certain fruits may replace a can of vegetables DEPENDING on their caloric value.*
>
> *Tomorrow I will calculate the exact caloric value I will be taking in each day and make some exercise ideas!*
>
> *Until then,*

STAY THIN!"

The glee that I can hear in my writing alarms me now; that I took such pleasure in the prospect of hurting and depriving myself makes me want to cry.

I am especially saddened when I listen to the tone in the next post, that I wrote less than 24 hours later. This one I called, 'Fat!'

"So, it only took me a day to ruin it. I'm coming home from therapy after only having green beans and spinach today and I felt so weak. I AM WEAK. A WEAK FAT DISGUISTING SON OF A BITCH. I ate a slice of cheesecake and then came home and ate carrot cake.

I then had every intention of booting it until I figured out that my throat will barely open because of my fucking jawbone. I still managed to force some of the carrot cake out. Tomorrow my punishment will be no food. I just need to break my stomach. This bastard fat ass will not keep me from puking just by a fucking jaw pain. You don't want to puke you fucking pussy? Fine then you just won't get the privilege of food."

My jaw was in pain because I'd just had my wisdom teeth removed. Hearing my self-abuse frightens me. The way that I separated my physical being and mental will into two separate beings is terrifying; it allowed me to punish my physical body, without feeling like I was hurting myself. I was trying to subordinate my cravings; I had to forget that the flesh and bone that was so 'needy' was a real part of me; I had to forget it was me.

It is hard for people who have not experienced an eating disorder to understand the extent to which the afflicted suffer. While desiring thinness is certainly a factor, it is not the illness as a whole, or even close. Like alcoholism or pathological gambling, it is an addiction that is entwined with both behaviors and physical sensations.

Let's be honest, no one thinks that it's healthy to shove two fingers down your throat to physically eject the food you just ate, but we tell *ourselves the end justifies the means and that our happiness lies in confining our physical expanse to an ever-decreasing amount of space; an ever-shrinking number on a scale.*

I felt overwhelmed by my life, by the changes that were happening within me, and on me, and I thought that in some twisted way if I could make myself smaller I could make everything stay the way I wanted. I felt so sick inside, and wanted to look sick outside, as well.

Of course the answer to being mentally ill isn't making your self physically ill. Eating disorders are not glamorous; it is exhausting to be consumed by thoughts of calories and weight; it is scary to be overpowered by urges to fast, binge and purge.

It is depressing to pull back into a world that feels all of your own; where you make all the rules and yet none ever make sense.

{ 14 }

Pills

The covers were pulled up over my head.

Perhaps I can will myself into not being here.

It didn't work.

When I pulled the covers down enough to peep around the room, I looked straight into my dad's face.

He was still standing there next to my bed, and his voice continued; his speech didn't falter.

"You're going to tell us whose house you were at," he said. "And there's no way we're sending you to Costa Rica after this."

Why won't he stop?

I began to cry.

"We'll talk about it in the morning," he said, almost sweetly, before making his way out of my room and then lightly closing the door.

Feeling sorry for myself, I sat in my bed sobbing for a few more minutes. I was quite drunk, and I knew that I should just go to bed.

But, I didn't.

Instead, I walked to the bathroom. I had to pee and suddenly felt the beer sloshing around my bloated stomach; it felt so heavy. My body wanted to expel it.

I locked myself in the bathroom and I looked at myself in the medicine cabinet mirror.

As I stared fiercely at my own reflection, I was so furious at that 'thing' that looked back at me. I felt distanced from that physical being, from that person who came home so drunk he was unable to go undetected like everyone else who had been at the party.

Worthless.

Opening the cabinet, I grabbed the first bottle of pills I saw.

I read the label.

The bottle belonged to my mother; it was her prescription of Welbutrin. I unscrewed the top and there were plenty of pills inside.

I can end all of this, I thought. *But, is it actually at the point where this is worth ending?*

I wondered: *What forces are propelling me toward this bathroom? What is making me consider taking my own life?*

I was not sad that I could no longer go to Costa Rica, and I was not sad that I had gotten into trouble.

Actually, I realized, *I am not that sad about much anything at all.*

It was much worse than that: It was emptiness. It was day after day of mindless floating; of going through the motions and waiting for the other shoe to drop.

It's as though I'd been operating as a ghost for the prior six months.

I was a good faker, I knew, and, aside from my parents, I didn't think people had been overly concerned about me. My grades had been nearly perfect; and I'd still maintained my friendships. I'd lost weight and often got too drunk, but if someone wasn't looking too closely I might have appeared relatively well adjusted.

Of course, I knew better; I knew myself. If there's one feeling that had not disappeared during this mostly apathetic trance it was my self-hatred.

I hated myself for so many things; for the things I had done, and the things I hadn't done; for who I was, and for who I wasn't.

I hated myself for sleeping with my friend's boyfriend, and I hated myself for falling in love with an older boy who I knew I could have momentarily, but never actually. I was sad that I gave myself to them; that I allowed them to take me; I gave one my mind and one my body, and I was not quite sure I'd ever feel like either of those aspects of my being would ever feel as though they were my own again.

I hated myself for being jealous of my straight friends. I felt it so unfair that they all didn't have to sleep with people secretly, or worry about being outed. I watched them flirt all day. Their budding sexualities, I was sure, were not simple, but everything they were going through was normal. I was furious I was not on this mainstream path of sexual discovery.

I hated myself for not being strong; I despised myself for not coming out publicly and paving the way for others who would come after me.

I hated myself for being so shallow, for spending days fasting and hours purging. For caring about whether I weighed 120 pounds or 130. I hated myself for constantly calculating my BMI, and for counting every calorie. I hated myself for still not being thin enough.

Things might get better, I told myself.

I couldn't imagine this might actually be true.

I tried to think of myself as a happy adult.

What would that look like for me? What would actually make you feel joy?

No images emerged. I couldn't think of what type of person I might like to marry, or what type of job I might like to have, or even where I might like to live.

My inability to conjure any vision of my ideal future self frightened me. Perhaps this meant I had already given up; perhaps this meant it really was my time to go.

I second-guessed this inclination, but the alcohol was overpowering.

Do it, I nagged myself. *Do it now. End your suffering.*

I poured a handful of the pills into my hand. They were so light in weight and crisply white; they were perfect little circles.

I moved my palm upward and shoved the pile of pills into my mouth. As soon as they were in, my saliva seemed to disappear. It was too big a pile to swallow.

After turning on the sink, I leaned over and filled my mouth with water.

Half of the pills went down with the first swallow, but the stubborn ones remained.

What if I just fall asleep?

No.

Impulsively, I grabbed the bottle of mouthwash sitting next to the sink. I ripped off its cap and filled my mouth with the stingingly fresh liquid. The pills released bubbles as they slowly disintegrated in the green anti-septic. I swallowed again, and the mouthwash and the pills hit my stomach.

I realized I was not half-assing this attempt; I was serious. I began chugging the bottle of mouthwash.

I'm going to die, I thought.

I opened the bathroom door, and I walked into the hall. My dad was standing there.

When I opened my mouth, I meant to speak, but instead projectile vomited. The hall echoed with the sound of clicks as the pills bounced around the floor.

My dad looked down and saw what had just burst from the center of my face. He began to shout, and I just kept throwing up.

***

When I woke up in the hospital, I was frankly surprised to be alive.

My mom and dad were in the room. Their expressions were the strangest hybrid of fear, anger and pity.

How am I here again?

Perhaps this all just a bad dream. Maybe if fall asleep, I will wake up and be back in my bed.

I tried to curl into a fetal position, but I instantly felt a sharp pain in my groin.

Not again.

The pain was stemming from where the catheter entered my body. I couldn't make such sudden movements.

I couldn't move much at all.

I felt poisoned; I was poisoned; I had poisoned myself.

Lying on my back, I cried like I had never cried before.

My body was convulsing; I was hyperventilating.

My dad came over and grabbed my arm. I couldn't even look at him. He squeezed hard.

I wondered what it must be like to be my parents. I figured they must feel caught between a desire to slap me and their mission to defend me from the big bad world.

You're wrong, I instantly told myself. *They don't want to protect you from the world; they want to protect you from yourself.*

The sound of footsteps grew nearer.

The nurse burst into the room; she was clearly agitated.

"He's awake?" she asked my parents, not even looking at me.

"Yes," my dad replied.

The nurse began shuffling around the small room. Barely glancing my way, she thrust a glass of water toward my huddled body.

I didn't take it; I closed my eyes and kept crying.

"I know you're sad," she said to me without looking. "But you've been here before. You should have learned the first time."

"He knows," my dad said, ever defensive.

The nurse left.

"I want to go home," I sobbed.

"They're keeping you for observation," said my dad.

"For how long?"

"A night."

"Why?" I begged. "Can't you make them let me go home?"

"You're a threat to yourself right now," he said. "You tried to kill yourself."

"I wasn't really trying to," I pleaded.

"Your blood alcohol content was even higher than last time."

"It was from the mouthwash," I offered.

"It doesn't matter," he said, sadly.

***

From the emergency room, I was wheeled to a new room.

The room was quiet; I was finally alone.

I spent most of the night sleeping, with nurses coming in and out to check on me.

I was glad to be away from the nurse from earlier.

"She pulled my catheter out aggressively on purpose," I told my dad.

"Maybe it was to get you back for throwing up all over the intake desk last night," he half-joked.

The nurses on my new floor were kinder; they spoke gently and moved around slowly.

They felt sorry for me.

Isn't sympathy what I wanted? I asked myself. *Then why does it make me feel so bad?*

"What floor is this?" I asked my dad.

"Psychiatric," he answered, looking away.

***

The doctor came into my room the next morning. He was young and handsome.

"I just need to ask you a few questions," he said. "But, first I want to say how lucky you are; there's another boy in the ICU who also overdosed on Welbutrin. Only he's in a coma."

I didn't feel lucky, so I didn't say anything. I just looked away, and felt a single tear run down my cheek.

"Did you really want to kill yourself?" he asked.

"No," I said, knowing it would make the aftermath of all of this much easier to brush aside.

"How do you feel now?"

"Shitty," I said, starting to cry again.

"Do you still want to hurt yourself?"

"No," I whispered. "I just want to go home."

He kept on asking me questions, and I kept on giving him short answers when I could find the room to breathe.

Finally, he started to get up. He offered me his hand to shake. I accepted.

"We'll send you home in a few hours," he said as he walked toward the door.

Just before leaving the room, he turned back around. His face grew stern and worried.

"Take care of yourself, Seamus."

***

I sat in a conference room with my parents at Meryl's office.

"I think it's time we look into inpatient rehab," she said. "This only seems to be escalating."

"When would he go?" my dad asked.

"Today or tomorrow," Meryl said. "Nothing good comes from waiting."

My parents looked right at me.

For a moment I made eye contact, but I couldn't hold it. I looked away.

"Seamus?" my mom asked.

I was in my head.

I don't want to be here anymore. I don't want to go back to school. I don't want to see my friends. Maybe going away will make me better. Maybe a break is what I truly need.

"Seamus?" my mom asked, again, louder this time.

I could now see my fate: Where some people have big parties or are surprised with new cars, I was going to celebrate my Sweet 16 with a stint in rehab.

"It will just be ten days," Meryl assured me. "Insurance won't cover any more than that."

I consented. I was miserable and reckless; I hated myself; I wanted an escape; I wanted a reprieve.

"Fine," I said.

Meryl smiled.

"I'll make some calls."

{ 15 }

Rehabilitation

I am not like you people.

"Do you drink every day?"

"No."

"Do you wake up covered in your own throw up?"

"Not usually."

"Do you do lots of drugs?"

"No...I've just smoked weed."

"Then what are you even doing here?"

Good question, I thought to myself. My expression remained blank.

The group was not satisfied; the faces kept staring at me; they wanted an answer.

Once it was clear I wasn't going to give them one, the group moderator, Bob – who I'd had an individual counseling session with earlier that day – cleared his throat:

"When he drinks he *really* drinks."

The crowd was unconvinced.

Bob sighed, "He's been hospitalized multiple times for alcohol poisoning."

Shrugs and nods served as confirmations that I had, in some way, met the group's unofficial requirements.

***

My therapist, Meryl, had chosen a youth lodge in the forested hills of middle-of-nowhere, Pennsylvania. It was a facility that she had worked with before; it was a facility that would accept my insurance.

As my dad drove me out, my heart sank to levels I did not know it could descend.

For most of the ride we were quiet. When our printed-out Map Quest directions suggested we were an hour away, we pulled off the highway to have lunch at a Friendly's.

As I ripped apart a chicken quesadilla that was simmering hot and slippery with oil, I fought back my tears.

"I don't want to go anymore," I said. I was scared, but I didn't want to let it show, so I defaulted to my icy tone.

"You've gotta go," my dad said. "You've committed; you promised."

***

From the moment I crossed the threshold, I could tell Babbling Creek was no respite.

The intake process was intense; one counselor grilled me about my drinking tendencies as another employee tore apart my bag.

"Did you bring alcohol with you?" the counselor asked.

I shook my head 'no,' as I could no longer formulate words; my tears could have filled an aquarium.

"What about drugs?"

I shook my head again.

"Well you can't have this," the other employee said as she pulled a small container of hand sanitizer from my duffel bag and threw it into the trash.

***

When I was allowed out of the office to say goodbye to my dad, I mustered the strength to whimper, "Please take me home."

He put his hand on my shoulder and let it rest, firmly; his pupils were gaping and his mouth became a straight thin line; he looked like he was burying my casket, not leaving me for ten days in Pennsylvania.

"You need this," he said. "We don't know what else to do."

***

The first activity I participated in took place in the gymnasium, a large building that sat about 100 yards from the main residential and administrative lodge.

I followed the group of close to 100 teenagers, starkly separated by gender – a rule that was strictly enforced. We climbed the stairs to what would have been a sound box in an actively used gym, but here had been transformed into a sort of group TV room.

We were made to sit crossed-legged on the floor; the girls made two rows in the front, with a large space separating them from the eight rows of boys behind them. The supervising staff members flanked us in chairs.

There would be no tomfoolery here.

We sat crossed-legged like kindergartners during story time, as the supervising staff pulled out a cart holding a TV and VCR that looked exactly like the ones that would always miraculously appear in elementary school classrooms on the days we had substitute teachers.

The lights went out, and a baseball themed episode of, *Touched by Angel*, started playing.

This is going to be so bizarre, I thought to myself as I looked around the room of engrossed teens.

This is going to be so bizarre, I thought to myself as I allowed myself to be engrossed, as well, and felt kind of sad and not ready when the episode ended.

***

"Hi, my name is Dan and I'm an addict. I'm from Bath, Pennsylvania and my drugs of choice are pills," said the bearded boy with the eyebrow piercing.

"Hi my name is Adam and I'm addict. I'm from Binghamton and my drugs of choice are Ecstasy and alcohol," said the next boy, who was lanky and wearing a polo.

As they went around the circle, I started trying to guess their drugs of choice before they confessed.

Next, a boy with a shaved-head and a Slipknot hoodie.

Weed.

"Hi my name is Evan and I'm an addict. I'm from Wilkes-Barre and my drugs of choice are alcohol and pills."

Damnit.

A suburban teen-queen, petite blonde; definitely a cheerleader.

Alcohol.

"Hi, my name is Lindsay and I'm an addict. I'm from Maine and my drug of choice is dope."

Jesus Christ. Heroin?!

An Italian girl with a New Jersey accent; Meadow Soprano's doppelgänger.

Coke.

"Hi my name is Krista and I'm an addict. I'm from Bergen County, New Jersey and my drug of choice is coke."

Bingo.

Before long, it was almost my turn.

But, first it was my roommate's.

"Hi my name is Rick, and I'm an addict. I'm from outside of Pittsburgh, and my drugs of choice are alcohol, weed, pills and coke."

My turn.

All eyes were on me; I was the new kid.

"Hi my name is Seamus and I'm an addict," I said, the words sounding like my lines for a play. "I'm from Syracuse, New York and my drug of choice is alcohol."

The girls smiled and the counselor nodded; I sounded fragile and weak; I sounded timid; I was scared.

***

Most of my fellow patients were court-ordered placements, and though I had avoided legal troubles, I was seeking lighter sentencing, in my own way, as well. My parents had let me know the consequences I would suffer if I didn't change my behavior. But the risk of losing a class trip to Costa Rica, my driver's permit and general teenage freedom did not curb my desire to disobey, my lust to self-destruct.

As we sat at folding card tables in the gymnasium during recreation time, or conversed as we walked laps around the basketball cart during some bizarre variation of peer recovery speed dating, I learned that many in my cohort had no plans to stay sober – and I can't say that I did either. Like them, I went through the motions; I shared in groups when I had to, and I forced myself to write letters to my family and my friends as though I wanted to change. I did not have a parole officer riding my ass, but I still had plenty of people who I didn't want hyper-scrutinizing my every action

***

While the other boys played basketball and volleyball, I sat at a table teaching myself chemistry, so I wouldn't be behind when I got back to school. Plus, I'd figured out that I was in second place for class rank, and I needed to get to first; I wanted to go to Brown.

"What the hell are you doing?" one boy asked me.

"My chemistry homework," I responded.

"You're still in school?" he said.

"Yeah," I asked, my head slightly cocked. "Aren't you?"

"Nah," he said.

"Oh," I said. *Fuck, this is awkward.*

"You're smart?"

"I don't know…I guess."

Silence.

Me floundering: "Why?"

"Some of the other guys are still in school," he said. "Maybe you can help them with math and shit."

"Yeah, of course. Just tell them to ask me."

***

My roommate, Rick, had gotten in trouble for dealing. He was then legally mandated to check into rehab.

"How long are you here?" he whispered to me at night as we lay in our beds in the room. The door was left ajar, and the night counselor, Doc, patrolled the hallways, making sure no one got into any trouble or tried to run away.

"Ten days," I said.

"That sucks, you seem easy to live with," he responded. "I guess I'll have to get a new roommate, hopefully he's not a fucking psycho like the last one."

I almost asked what had made the former inhabitant of my bed come to be known as a "psycho," but I wanted to sleep soundly. Though I was notoriously nosey, I was slowing learning that sometimes ignorance truly is bliss.

***

Most of the counselors were middle-aged men, but one woman, Stacy, was about 35 and shapely. I certainly wouldn't have nominated her to be the next Miss Pennsylvania, but she wore tight fitting pantsuits and blouses, and didn't have a potbelly, ill-fitting slacks or a penis like the five other counselors. Thus, comparatively, I guess I can see why the other boys lusted after her more than Eve had craved a bite of that damn apple. Besides, they were allowed to talk to Stacy, unlike the female patients, whose rooms were located in a wing off the far side of the lobby.

One day, I sat with a group of boys, during the recreation period.

"Yo, sometimes during my sessions I swear Stacy wants me," the bearded boy Dan, said. "I wanna bend her over like *bam-bam-bam.*"

"Yo, when is the last time you had sex?" asked a skater boy, Tim, who I had grown close with.

"Like two months ago with my girl right before I got arrested," Dan said. "What about you, man?"

"Yeah like two weeks ago with my girl," replied Tim.

"Wow, I miss my girl," Dan said.

"Me too, man. Mine is a little older, she's 19," Tim bragged. "I went up to visit her at college and we spent the whole weekend fucking in the shower."

"Wow, what I would give," Dan sighed, shaking his head.

"And she gives the best head," Tim continued. "When she deep throats..."

"My girls got her clit pierced," Dan divulged. "And I've got my Prince Edward done, she loves riding that shit."

"Wait, what's a Prince Edward?" I asked, joining the conversation.

Dan took the tip of his thumb and rested it against the top of the bottom knuckle on his pointer finger creating a diagram of male anatomy.

"I have a piercing here," he said pointing to the tip of his pointer finger. "And I have one here," he continued, pointing to where his would be shaft joined his would be scrotum.

"Oh, wow," I responded. "That sounds painful."

"What was painful for me is now pleasurable as shit for her."

***

The architecture of the lodge was pretty odd. When you walked in, you entered a large, open octagon shaped lobby. There were floor to ceiling windows, wooden paneling and dusty red carpets that were undoubtedly installed in the 1970s. Generic red-cushioned futon-like-couches with light wood arm rests were scattered in clusters throughout the open space. A piano sat in the corner.

"This is where we sing carols during our Christmas party," my counselor had told me during my initial tour.

Shit, that's depressing.

The lobby had eight doors; one led outside, four led to administrative offices, and three opened into three long hallways; two held the boys' rooms and one belonged to the girls. The nurse's office was at the end of the girls' hallway, so us boys had to go outside and walk around every morning so we could stand in a long line to get our prescription medications.

"Show me your mouth," the nurse would say, making sure we weren't stashing pills beneath our tongues. As we walked back to the lodge, the boys would stare wistfully at girls' windows.

"One time I saw Britt without a bra in the bathroom."

"I bet mad lesbian shit goes on over there."

***

All of the bedrooms had two doors; one opened to the hallway and one opened to a bathroom that was also connected to the bedroom next door. This architectural arrangement quickly proved to be quite problematic for me.

My roommate, Rick, wasn't especially well liked; he tried too hard to impress people; he wanted to seem dominant, but just came off as a wannabe. He hated the boy, Mark, who lived in the room on the other side of our shared bathroom.

During the day, when the counselors weren't looking, they would smack each other, and a few times, their horseplay nearly led to real blows.

Mark clearly had behavioral issues – if not developmental disabilities – and was definitely not receiving all of the services he needed at this rather rudimentary institution.

"Hey, Rick," he called through the bathroom.

"What do you want, dickhead?" Rick shouted back.

"You're a motherfucking faggot," Mark called back, shrieking with laughter.

"Yo, I swear to God I'm gonna fuck him up," Rick said to me.

I widened my eyes; I wanted to leave before a conflict broke out, but we were confined to our rooms to clean. I'd already vacuumed, and Rick had taught me how to make my bed with tight corners, like one would do in the army.

I heard someone stirring in the bathroom. There was the sound of objects being shifted, and then a splash.

"You're gonna what?" Mark challenged.

"I'm gonna fuck you up!" Rick responded, his voice now ravaged by rage.

Mark burst into the room swinging the sopping wet plunger. He charged toward Rick's bed, a devilish grin on his face.

Rick popped up and swung at Mark, but Mark glided past him smearing the plunger all over his pillows.

I cringed, but Rick wanted blood. He swung at Mark harder than I'd ever seen anyone hit before. His fist connected with the back of Mark's head, and the plunger fell from his hands and rolled on the floor.

Mark's eyes crossed for a moment. Rick tried to capitalize on the moment of confusion he lunged for the plunger, but Mark regained focus and open-palmed slapped the back of Rick's neck.

I could feel the sting from across the room.

Mark spun on his heels and ran across the room toward the bathroom. Rick began to pursue but Mark was faster. He got back into his own room, slammed the door shut, and parked his desk chair right in front of the door to create a barricade, which he must have reinforced with his body weight.

Rick pounded on the door, and threw his body weight against it, but it didn't budge. On the other side, an overall victorious Mark cackled like a hyena. Rick threw himself against the door one last time then gave up. He knew better than to create such a ruckus that a counselor would come by.

He marched back into the room from the bathroom.

"He's gonna regret that," he promised himself, hissing into the room's stifled air.

***

The next afternoon, when I came back to my room from lunch, Rick and his friend, Dave, were standing in the few feet between my bed and the bathroom door.

As I walked in, they both shot their heads toward the door.

"Oh, it's just you," Dave said.

"Just me."

"Rick, do it now," Dave said. "I swear I saw him go into his individual session."

"Watch the hall," said Rick as he walked into the bathroom, locking the door behind him.

"What's he doing?" I asked.

"If I tell you, then you're technically an accomplice," Dave cooed.

"Okay. Don't tell me then," I said.

"Man, hurry up!" Dave yelled to Rick.

"I need a porno or something, dude," Rick called back.

"Just hurry up. Don't get stage fright."

"Alright. Shut the fuck up, dude. You're distracting me."

Dave stayed glue to the doorframe, his head peeping out into the hallway just enough to be able to see all the way down into the lounge.

The toilet flushed and the door to the bathroom unlocked. Rick reemerged; a bottle of v05 strawberry moisture milk shampoo was in his hand.

"Look at this, man," he said holding the bottle out. Dave started to walk over, and curiosity got the best of me as I inched toward the bottle, as well.

The shampoo was pink and glistened under the overheard light; it had a slick texture, but something was congealing on the top of liquid's surface; something glossy and gooey; semen.

"Oh my god, ew," I said, stomach retching. "You did not just 'cum' in his shampoo."

"Don't fucking tell anyone," Rick said, marking the first time he had ever spoken to me with that tone he so frequently directed at other people.

"I'm not going to," I replied.

But if I did, you wouldn't be around long enough to do anything about it.

"Alright, shake the shit up and put it back," Dave said to Rick. "I'm sure Mark's getting out any second."

***

I didn't really understand why Rick had been so adamant about me not telling anyone. For the rest of the day, whenever I was around him or Dave, they couldn't have been more eager to divulge every detail of their dirty trick.

***

That night, as we were getting ready for bed, the door from the bathroom flew open and crashed against the wall. Mark came in swinging something around his head. The helicopter effect outwardly spread the venomous stench of something rotting; the room was filled by the smell of waste. Human waste.

"What the fuck," Rick shouted, backing up. "CHILL!"

"You popped a nut in my fucking shampoo?" Mark seethed. "Well, I didn't use it because your fucking big mouth beat you at your own game."

He slowed down his swinging, and I was able to see that he had a discolored tube sock in his hand. As the sock's motion ceased, and it limply dangled from his fist, the smell continued to spread.

Shit, I thought. *He shit in that sock.*

I was sitting on my bed; my hand was over my mouth and nose. I crab crawled backward, until I was pressed against the wall. I prayed that any mishap did not leave me with feces strewn across my face.

Mark started swinging again as he quickly moved toward Rick.

"STOP!" Rick screamed, actively disregarding whatever de facto code they'd established to avoid adult intervention.

This failed subtle attempt at snitching – a flagrant violation of peer code – only served to further infuriate Mark.

He lunged toward Rick, as he lassoed the sock-full-of-shit zipping above his head. Then, like a viper, he made he move; he tried to strike.

But, Rick saw it coming, he ducked and the sock hit the wall.

PLOP.

It left a filthy smear on the wall and like a stink bomb, the impact made the stench utterly putrid, intolerable.

Mark pulled back his arm to swing again, but then froze as a counselor's gruff voice filled the hall.

"What the hell is going on back there?"

Fast footsteps. He was approaching.

"Shit," Mark said. "Shit. Fuck. Shit."

"Throw it out the fucking window you retard!" said Rick.

Mark ran over to the window next to my bed, and I lifted it open, not wanting his soiled fingers to touch anything so close to my bed. He chucked the sock out onto the grass and I slammed the window shut.

He sprinted back through the bathroom, just as a counselor reached the door to his room, on the other side.

"What's all this noise?" the counselor asked. "And what's that smell?"

"Nothing," Mark said. "The toilet was clogged but we fixed it."

"Yeah," the counselor said voice lowering to a growl. "Better be fixed."

***

"Seamus, I have great news for you!" my counselor, Bob, exclaimed as I entered his office. "Please, sit down."

I sat across from him in the small wooden paneled office that looked like it belonged on a cheesy yacht from 1960's Miami Beach. It was disorganized; piles of papers were everywhere, and he had too many knick-knacks; I felt ill at ease.

"So, your insurance has decided to extend your stay for 30 days," he gleefully announced.

The blood drained from my face and fire spread through my cheeks. I didn't know whether I wanted to scream or cry; whether I should shout "no," or try to run away in the middle of the night.

"Oh," I said, flatly. "Okay, great."

I forced the corner of my mouth to feign an empty smile.

Bob didn't notice. He had already begun sifting through a stack of paper that he had pulled out from beneath an overflowing box.

I sat for a minute later, and he looked up from his work with a smile.

"Good, good, good," he whistled. "See ya later."

***

I was going home.

30 days had passed, and it was finally my time to go. So soon would I be back to in my house, back at school, back with my family and back with my friends.

But, I knew everything would be different.

At least initially, I supposed, *everyone will treat me like I was sick at best, like a social leper, at worst.*

I couldn't think about that now. I would have to deal with that when I was back. I would figure out a way to normalize all of this craziness; it had always worked in the past.

I needed to be present. I was in the gym, and it was almost my turn to speak.

The patients and the counselors sat in one section of folding chairs, while my parents and the family members of the other patients who were leaving sat in a separate, but nearly adjacent, section.

Before we went home, we were made to give an emotional presentation of sorts. We had to speak of the mistakes we now recognized we had made in the past; we had to share what we'd learned at rehab.

There had been moments that I'd bought in, that I'd almost believed I might actually be a sick as some of these other kids, but ultimately, I knew I would eventually return to partying.

Partying is fun. It makes me happy.

Yet, when my turn came, I knew what I had to say. I nervously made my way to the front of the room, and stared off at no one in particular.

In the real world, I competed in - and won - public speaking contests. I enjoyed the high from delivering cutting speeches about constitutional issues. I could sound like a lawyer; I could be impressive.

But, here, I just wanted to get through it as quickly as possible.

So I began, my voice shaking:

When I got here, I guess I didn't realize how sick I was. My drinking was ruining my life. I'd been to the hospital twice, and almost died both times. I was being unfair to my friends and family, and choosing alcohol over them. I am excited to continue my sobriety, and become apart of the AA community in Syracuse.

People clapped, and my parents smiled.

I felt a pang of guilt, as I knew I didn't truly mean any of what I had just said.

I assumed, on some level, my parents were aware I was just going through the motions, as well.

{ 16 }

Outpatient

"I'd like to go around and have everyone introduce themselves, and just briefly explain why they're here," said the grandmotherly woman who sat with us patients in the semi-circle of chairs.

The woman was Meryl's employee; she was the facilitator of my twice-a-week outpatient program.

In the room sat 15 other patients; 14 of them were adults, and just one boy was a teenager, like me.

I was so nervous about sharing my own story; I still didn't believe that I belonged there in that room with those people.

I am always in the wrong place at the wrong time. I'll be fine in the long run, I believed.

These other people, they must be real addicts; addicts on another level, like the kids with me at rehab.

Almost all of them are so old. They must have done awful things; they must have done irreparable damage in their own lives.

An elderly man sat to the right of the facilitator.

When no one else spoke, he began.

"My name is Kenneth," he said.

"Hi, Kenneth," said everyone else in unison.

"I forgot to add one thing," interjected the facilitator. "Part of being in this group means going to meetings, so I'd like you to introduce yourself as you would at a meeting."

"Hello, my name is Kenneth, and I'm an alcoholic," Kenneth said.

"Hi, Kenneth," everyone else repeated.

"I'm 60 years old. I'd been drinking every day for decades, and I'd gotten several DUIs and ruined jobs," he said. "But, I finally decided it was actually time to become sober when my daughter stopped talking to me."

His life sounds so bleak, I thought. *I'm nowhere near that place.*

"Hi, my name is Mary, and I'm an alcoholic," said the pretty, thirty-something-year-old woman who spoke next

"Hi, Mary," sang the chorus.

"I was having an affair with a younger man, and began to get out of control," she said. "He started calling in the middle of the night, and he would leave bags of cocaine beneath my windshield wipers as gifts. I'm a mother and a wife and when the guilt caught up to me I tried to drive my car full speed into a pole while I was high."

She paused for a moment.

"I am also here for my son," she said.

The facilitator interrupted.

"But, are you also here for yourself?" she asked.

Mary didn't answer immediately. She closed her eyes and took a deep breath.

Why does this require such deep thinking? It's either yes or no.

"Well, yes," Mary said. "I guess I am here for myself, as well."

Next, a woman who physically reminded me of my own mother told her story.

"Hi, my name is Lydia, and I'm an alcoholic," she said, sounding pained as she announced the last part.

"I just finished treatment at rehab," she said. "I've been drinking every day for years, and I pretended I'd stopped several times. But, I decided to admit to myself that I needed help after my husband realized I'd been filling mouthwash bottles with vodka that I'd dyed green."

It was my turn.

Everyone else has been so honest, I thought. *I need to volunteer details, or else they'll just ask for more.*

"Hi, my name is Seamus, and I'm an alcoholic," I said quickly.

No matter how many times I'd had to say it at inpatient, it always felt so foreign coming from my lips. I feared I was transparent; that my inauthenticity might show through as though my intentions were as transparent as a clean pane of glass.

"I just got out of inpatient rehab," I continued, my voice quavering. "I went because I'd had alcohol poisoning once, and then had to be hospitalized again for taking pills and chugging mouthwash while drunk."

The members of the group looked sympathetic; they looked as though they understood.

I panicked as I wondered if I might actually be like them.

Are my crimes so different than their own?

{ 17 }

Relapse

"Okay, I'm going to the movies," I shouted to my dad.

"Alright," he said, from the dining room.

I heard the ruffling of the newspaper as he turned to the next page.

Like a statue, I stood still, waiting for a suspicious question.

But, none came.

It had been nearly three months since I'd left rehab.

For the first month, he'd been hyper-vigilant.

During that period, he'd made me let him talk to my friends' parents before I went to their houses.

One night, he even randomly showed up at friend's house to "drop off candy," which I knew was to make sure a parent was home and that I wasn't drinking.

I had been furious, but I hadn't fought.

I was smart enough to know that the best way to get them to loosen their hold was to behave. If I acted out, they'd realize I was still the same damaged human.

It had worked.

As I walked out the door, I already felt victorious.

I had a full three hours before I had to be home, and I was going to make use of them.

I was 16-years-old and on my way to the 21st birthday party of a girl I had lifeguarded with that past summer before rehab.

Between the month at rehab, the outpatient program, and the increased parental surveillance, I'd felt I'd paid my dues. I'd taken time off, and I thought I would now be fine to return to drinking.

One drink, I told myself. *Tonight you can finally have that one drink.*

***

One drink never really was one drink.

Even after all of my experiences, that night was no exception.

I fell right back in where I'd left off.

The party was full of kids much older than me. I felt awkward and self-conscious.

I wanted to be drunk and carefree.

So I pursued those feelings.

I smoked weed, and took shots. I never was without a beer.

Nobody here knew about rehab like all of my friends in high school. No one here cared what I was doing.

I thought that falling back into drunkenness would feel so dramatic. I thought my body might resist crossing back over that invisible boundary.

But, it didn't.

Instead, every cell of my being seemed to embrace my return.

Once I cracked open that first beer, and had that first sip, I didn't feel guilty, I felt good.

More, more, more, my desire echoed through my body.

Suddenly, I realized I was quite drunk.

It felt lovely.

I moved to the corner of the living room full of smoke, where I began talking to the birthday girl.

"I want to make out with somebody," I heard myself say.

"I'll make out with you," she said giggling.

"Okay," I said, the proposition sounding totally normal.

So we did.

Our lips came together, and then our mouths opened and tongues danced across each other.

There was no sexual attraction; there was just a mutual desire to be wild.

Free spirit, I thought. *I am just a trapped free spirit.*

After ten seconds the realization that we were making out set in. I burst out laughing, and then she did, as well.

I wanted another drink.

{ 18 }

A+

At the end of every marking period, the list of honors students ranked by their grade point averages was posted on the wall.

Every day, after school, I would walk past the glass cabinet to check if the list had been updated.

I'd scan until I found my name.

Usually it did not take long, as I was almost always at the top.

In middle school, I'd been a fine student, but once I got to high school I'd realized I could be the best.

What was more fulfilling than being the best?

I'd decided I was going to go to Brown University; I would do whatever it took to get in. I was obsessed with the idea of going to an Ivy League school. No one in my family had ever gone to one.

I worked my ass off. I stayed up all night doing homework. I pored over books, and stayed after school to review concepts I had trouble understanding with teachers.

When my grades weren't perfect, I would freak out. I'd put that much more manic energy into the next test or project.

I knew I was fucked up in other areas of my life, so academics became the space where I would reign.

The more I excelled in school, the more I wanted to rebel outside of it.

"You have the most imbalanced personality of anyone I've ever met," my dad told me one morning after I'd come home sloppily drunk after getting a nearly perfect report card. "You can't just do whatever you want."

"I'm doing everything I need to be doing," I whined, trying to get out of trouble. "I'm not even barely doing it, I'm excelling."

He sighed; he couldn't argue with that.

{ 19 }

Snapped

"What are you on?" my mom demanded.

We were in the kitchen, and I turned away from her, trying desperately to hide my pilled out state.

"Nothing," I said, the words coming out so slowly. I needed to make sure I remained articulate, though my voice sounded grossly delayed.

"You must think we're stupid," she said. "I know you came home drunk last night, and I know you're high on something right now."

"No I'm not," I said, the words inching out of my mouth; they felt like slugs that I might be able to grip with my fingers and extract from beneath my tongue.

"Your pupils are huge," she seethed.

"No, they're not," I made one last pathetic attempt at defense. "Leave me alone."

"Why do you keep doing this?"

"Stop!"

"Do you need to go back to rehab?" she asked. "Do you want to go back to rehab?"

"No," I screamed.

I began to feel myself boil over.

"Then why do you keep doing this?" she screamed, overwhelmed with frustration.

Why won't she just stop?

Her voice continued, but I couldn't even make out the words she was saying anymore. The sound was giving me a headache. I could tell I was about to go crazy

I took a deep breath.

The noise hadn't stopped.

"JUST SHUT UP," I yelled. My anger surprised me. I was about to break down.

Her voice grew louder.

"Shut up?" she yelled. "You're going to tell ME to shut up right now?"

I snapped.

I grabbed a knife from the knife block and held it to my wrist.

"I'll do it," I yelled, completely out of my mind.

She started screaming for my dad; she was sobbing.

I put the knife down on the counter and turned and ran out the front door.

***

The streets were a blur as I ran; I was running through my childhood neighborhood like a madman.

What would I think if I saw myself? I thought. *I would probably be freaked out.*

I quickened my pace.

I have gone crazy; I have lost my mind; I have snapped.

Snapping is such a strange sensation; like skydiving, you move to the edge of sanity and then sit there, your legs dangling. 'Once you're half out, you may not be able to come back in,' you've been told, but you still hover on the edge, undecided. Then, you push yourself forward, or you drop by accident, but, either way, you're suddenly falling faster than you ever knew it was possible to fall.

The farther you drop the more momentum you gain; the insanity fans itself.

It was dark, and I kept moving; I kept speeding through the streets by foot.

What would I do if I stop? I can't go home.

Headlights approached.

I tried to hide, but the car sped toward me and then stopped right next to me.

The window rolled down, and my mom's friend was behind the wheel.

I made eye contact as I ran past.

"Seamus!" she yelled. "Get in the car."

I looked at her, and I thought about getting in the car. My pace slowed for a moment.

I've already gone too far.

I turned and sprinted away.

"Seamus!" she commanded. "Get back here."

The shouts faded behind me. I stayed in the shadows and lengthened my stride.

***

I didn't know where else to go besides the reservoir.

I'll go to the water tower and sit. Up there, on the hill above the city, it will be quiet.

Normally, I would have been afraid to navigate the terrain alone at night. There weren't many lights on the acres of isolated land.

What if someone crazy is there? I usually would have thought before deciding against moving through the darkness on my own.

But, on that night, that was not my thought process.

On that night, I was crazy too.

***

My friend picked me up in her car from the corner of the reservoir's sprawling lawn.

We just drove around, hardly speaking.

I wished I could cry, or that I could explain why I felt so over-whelmed, but I couldn't. I was expressionless and flat; I couldn't even fake an emotion.

I just stared out the window.

My friend's phone began to ring.

"Oh, shit, Seamus," she said. "It's your parents."

"Ignore it," I said, in a tone so icy it sent shivers down my own spine.

She did.

But, then they called again.

She ignored this second call.

Then they called again.

She answered.

"Hello," she said, her voice shaking.

The person on the line said something. I tried to listen, but I couldn't hear.

"No he's not with me...Okay, yes he is....Alright. I'll bring him there."

She hung up.

"I have to bring you to the Gannon's parking lot," she said. "Your parents are there, and they called the police."

***

When we got to the parking lot, I got out of the car.

The summer air was humid, and it reminded me of childhood nights I'd spent sleeping on a mattress we'd put on our screened-in balcony; those nights were so simple, but they'd always felt like ad-ventures.

Seeing the police walk toward me made brought me back to reali-ty.

My parents stood in the background, but I ignored them.

Traitors, I thought. *They should have known I would have moved on from this episode on my own.*

The officer approached me.

"Do you have any weapons?"

"No," I said, trying to appear composed, though my voice still sounded hollow and distant.

"Do you want to hurt yourself?"

"No," I said again.

"Okay, well we need you to come with us," the second officer said. "Will you cooperate?"

"Am I under arrest?"

"No," the first officer said. "You're not under arrest."

"Then where are we going?"

"We need to get you to a psychiatric evaluation," the second officer said.

"Fine," I sighed as I walked toward them, accepting that escaping was a fight I would never win.

"Okay," the second officer said, opening the back door of the police car. "Can you climb in here?"

I made my way to the car, walking with the best posture I could conjure. I tried to feign pride.

I climbed in the back seat and they closed the door behind me.

I was locked in.

***

It is always strange how quickly an experience becomes normalized.

I never thought I would find myself in the back of a police car, and yet there I was.

The seat felt harder than a normal car's seat; it felt more plastic, like a toy car had become life-sized.

Do they make these uncomfortable on purpose?

The officers tried speaking to me, but I glanced out the window and pretended I didn't hear.

I watched familiar neighborhoods appear and disappear through the window. They felt so far away.

The car pulled up to the gate at the local psychiatric hospital. The cops said something quietly to the guard, and the gates opened.

We pulled into the silent parking lot with its unsettling orange lights.

The officers got out first, and then they let me out.

One officer walked toward the door, and the other waited.

As I began moving, he followed behind me.

I acted as though I did not notice their flanking me; I acted as though I did not know they thought I might still be a threat.

***

"Are you going to hurt yourself?" the intake nurse asked for what felt like the millionth time.

"No," I said, exasperated. "All I want is to sleep."

"What happened tonight?"

"Can I please go home?" I asked. "I already have a therapist."

"You're spending the night here," she said. "We need to make sure you don't hurt yourself."

At this point, I didn't even care that I was being detained. The pills I'd popped were wearing off, and I feared I might fall asleep right there in the chair.

"Okay," I said. "Then can't I just sleep now and answer your questions in the morning?"

"Are you currently on drugs, Seamus?"

"I need to sleep."

***

The morning came so soon, and I woke up in my little secured cell.

What is wrong with me? How did I just sleep in this cell without trouble?

A nurse knocked on the door, and then entered.

"Hi, Seamus," she said. "The doctor would like to see you."

***

I went into the doctor's office.

He asked the same questions I'd already been asked, so many times over.

"Are you going to hurt yourself?"

"No."

"What drugs were you on?"

I paused. I could have told him about the different pills I had popped into my mouth; how the world instantly felt like it was moving in slow motion.

But, I didn't.

"I just smoked weed," I said. "I think it had something in it."

"We'd like to blood test you and see what's in your system," he said.

"Do I have to?"

He seemed surprised by my question.

"Well, no," he said. "I suppose you aren't legally bound."

I straightened my posture, and become a bit colder; more collected.

This was my leverage.

"Then I'd like to be released."

{ 20 }

Overachiever

Soon, I will be gone. Soon, I will be free. I will have no curfews, no watching parents, and no reputation. I will be able to do what I want.

I sat on a blanket in my friend's backyard. She lived around the corner from my parents' house, and a group of my closest friends were huddled together near a fire.

We roasted marshmallows and drank cans of Bud Light.

"We did it!" one of my best friends said. "We're done with high school."

He raised his can, and we all did the same. We clinked our drinks together, and said our cheers.

"And, Seamus, you killed it earlier," he said. "Ya damn nerd."

***

Earlier that night, I'd walked onto a stage as the valedictorian. In the past, there'd been issues with student speakers being interrupted during their speeches; crowd members had shouted that they should 'Wrap it up!'

Our school – which was massive, public and inner-city – had a graduation rate that hovered just above 50%. Each year, they held annual meetings for parents asking them to not interrupt or blow fog-horns during speeches.

The meetings never seemed to do the trick in the past.

But, earlier that night, I'd walked to the podium, to deliver my speech from memory.

I'd fallen into a rhythm, and the words had poured out of me. No one interrupted me, and rather I took command of the room of over 1,000 people. I felt their attention drawn toward me. I was so scared that I grew calm; I was so self-conscious, I grew proud.

The moment was powerful; I was powerful in the moment. It was euphoric. As I spoke people applauded, and gave standing ovations. It was a high unlike any other; a high so much better than being drunk.

In the graduation pamphlet, I was listed as the valedictorian, one of three class presidents, and the National Honor Society vice president. Next to my name it announced that I would attend Brown University; there were symbols demarcating that I'd earned every honor possible.

It was the end of a long leg of a race; the race to never fail; to win; to be perfect.

Despite these achievements, as I sat at that fire with my friends, I wanted nothing more than to escape this moment.

I wanted to be in the next phase of life. I wanted to be an adult, with autonomy and agency. I wanted to have a family, a house, and a career that came with power.

I was never happy where I was.

"Cheers to what's going to be an amazing summer," another friend said.

I raised my can and went through the motions, but I knew, were it possible, I was already ready to completely leave this summer behind.

{ 21 }

Excess

"How's everything going?" my dad asked over the phone. "Looks like you're having a ball from pictures."

I sat on the regal steps of one of Brown's original buildings on the Main Green. I had stared at pictures of these buildings longingly for so many years; I remembered walking past these steps while taking a tour of Brown, and praying that I might one day be hanging out there myself like the relaxed students had been that sunny spring day.

But, now everything looked different.

First of all, it was an early October night, and the dim lights reflected eerily through the lurking fog.

Second of all, my idyllic image of the school had been shattered.

"It's fine," I said, starting to choke up. "Actually, I don't think I like it very much here."

"What's wrong?" my dad asked.

What isn't wrong? I thought to myself. I couldn't help but picture the blackouts, the throwing up, the classes I'd already missed, the mornings and afternoons spent in bed nursing a hangover.

But, I couldn't tell him any of that.

So I just focused on the loneliness.

"Everyone is just so … rich," I said. "Everyone's always spending so much money and I just feel so broke all of the time. I hate it. And they all already know each other from summer camps, or they're family friends."

"College is an adjustment," my dad replied calmly. "You'll find your people."

How could I make him understand? Growing up, I'd always gone to inner-city schools where, relatively, I'd been the privileged one. I'd grown up recognizing that though my parents were always stressed about money, I still was afforded countless opportunities that my peers simply were not.

How could my dad, a normal person from lower middle-class America, comprehend kids running around with limitless credit cards? How could I explain how shitty it was to always be anxious I'd have to split some huge bill at the end of an extravagant meal? I was living off student loans, where these kids had bank accounts that seemed to have no bottom. The amount of money one had seemed to determine who your friends were; if you were always eating at the dining hall, you were in one world; if you never did, you were in another.

The differences had become immediate from the first day, when I moved my stuff in with my parents' old minivan, while many of my peers had car services and professional movers. The level of casual extreme wealth at Brown was shocking; it was something I had never even really known existed.

I hated the feeling of being 'less than;' the sense of being inadequate in any way.

In this elite environment, every day reminded me of screening calls from bill collectors as a child. When I checked my bank account I felt the same pit in my stomach I'd experienced listening to my parents fight about spending when I was little.

"I feel like they're all in a club that I don't belong to," I said.

My light crying turned into a heavy sobbing, as I allowed myself to admit that I was unhappy at my dream school. I felt on the outside; left out; a feeling that I had been convinced would disappear when I got to the college of my dreams.

"There are hundreds of kids like you there," my dad said. "Have you given yourself a break from partying?"

"Yeah," I said immediately, though I'd been heavily drunk at minimum four nights a week since arriving a month earlier.

"Why don't you try to cut back and really throw yourself into your classes?" he offered. "If you don't like it at the end of the semester, you can always transfer."

"Okay," I said, still crying.

"Are you okay?" he asked, concerned.

"I'll be fine," I said.

"Okay, well, seriously give yourself a break."

"I will," I said, "I'm just going to go watch a movie."

What I really wanted was a drink.

***

In part, my dad was right.

I did find my people.

But, he was partially wrong in that many of them were not from the same world as me.

As weeks passed, people began being honest about money. Those with limitless allowances curbed their behaviors to accommodate those of us who were not so fortunate. Other times, they just paid for everyone.

Where money and class had been the connecting points of my Ivy League social scene, alcohol was an even more powerful bridge.

Where people could not bond over similar economic lifestyles or upbringings, as "partiers" we could relate over our appreciation of getting fucked up.

I was always down to drink; I was always down to get drunk.

Thus, quickly, I made many friends.

I had my own currency: Wildness.

{ 22 }

Tripping

The walls were breathing; they had a pulse. The room slid back and forth on an invisible axis

It was not scary; it was soothing. I felt like I knew truth; I was wrapped in it.

Next to me Dalton – my friend with whom I occasionally hooked up – was not so at peace.

Moments before, he had ripped off his clothes as though they were aflame. Once stripped down to his underwear, he had curled into a fetal position.

He had become a baby. His voice changed and it sounded like it belonged to an infant rather than a grown man.

Did his trip make the octave change? Or has my mind made me imagine it sounds completely unrecognizable?

Every few minutes he poked his head up from his heap of limbs.

"When will this be over?" he asked. "Will I ever see my family again?

I laughed. That was all I could manage to do.

He looked at me, his eyes full of tears.

I couldn't help but feel unsympathetic; I couldn't help but feel like he could will himself to notice that everything now had a heartbeat. From my mattress to the desk chair, everything was alive.

How could he not see the magic that was happening around us? How could he find this space scary?

"Am I going to be like this forever?" he asked to no one in particular.

I tried to look away and ignore him, but the absurdity of his question made me begin to giggle. Eventually, a full bout of laughter grew inside of me and burst out of my throat.

"Just try to enjoy it," I was eventually able to spit out between my cackling. My words felt like they had physical boundaries as they formed; they felt like silk as they snaked over my lips and into the world.

I wouldn't mind staying like this forever, I thought. *The world feels much nicer this way.*

Perhaps, I had become a baby too. The difference was, I liked the feeling: The world felt like a womb; it felt so safe and warm.

"I want it to end," Dalton shouted.

"Shhh," I whispered.

We were likely only a quarter of the way into our trip.

Dalton was not the only who didn't like the feeling.

There were more people who took the mushrooms with us earlier, but slowly they had disappeared.

One felt too tall, and ran to her room.

Another felt as if he was dying. He said he could feel bugs on his skin.

I wonder why I feel so at peace, when most everyone else has responded so violently?

I did not doubt whether or not I would soon lose that feeling; I knew I would return to real life.

But, I wanted to enjoy it while I was there.

The air was so beautiful; I could see the air.

I watched it dance around the room.

"I don't like it!" Dalton yelled.

"Shhhh," I whispered. "I do."

{ 23 }

Action

"Can I have some?" I whined, no longer able to keep my eyes open.

There was a face in front of mine, and I was speaking to it; speaking at it. Yet, as soon as I made my request, I couldn't really remember exactly whom the face belonged to or precisely what I was trying to acquire.

"Just a little bit," the voice responded. "You're already drunk."

Who is that?

The voice was distinct, yet I just couldn't place it. All I could see was a blurry face and the dark outline of people moving around the field as the rap music made my inner ear vibrate.

I don't like it.

The person held their hand out in front of my face, and I saw a small purple pill resting in his palm.

He was waiting for me to grab it. Whatever it was - speed, Ecstasy, Adderall – I knew it would help me stay awake.

His fingers beckoned toward the pill in the floating palm; an offering. I could break a little piece off and give it all back.

But, I wanted it all.

Like one of Fisher Price's hungry hippos, I lunged my head forward and took the whole pill out of the person's hand with my teeth. I pulled it back with my tongue, and I bit down. I chewed the entire thing, my teeth grinding the pill into a powder that made me gag as an intense bitterness filled my mouth.

"Oh my God!" the person said, squealing with laughter.

***

"The Westin! The Westin!" I awoke to someone shouting.

I quickly realized that the raised voice belonged to myself.

I tried to conjure my last solid memory, but I couldn't seem to remember at all how I'd gotten there.

Were my body not in motion, I'd have been certain I'd just awoken from a deep sleep. But, I was bouncing off the walls of the cab in a way that would be impossible had I just been passed out.

The cab driver ignored me as he sped through College Hill toward downtown Providence. I wasn't wearing my seatbelt, and the sensation of being knocked around with each turn was exhilarating. I remembered the teacher in driver's ed telling horror stories of backseat passengers being 'projectiled' through the windshield, but at that moment I liked the feeling of risk. I was fascinated by the potential to fly.

When I turned to my right, I noticed there was a boy sitting right there, by my side. The boy was so close to me; I was almost sitting on him.

I couldn't quite recall who this boy was, and I was much too distracted by the jerks and turns of the taxi to try to figure it out. I put my hand on the boy's leg and he didn't move away; he started kissing me, instead.

I closed my eyes and kissed him back as I was thrown around like a rag doll by the driver's sudden twists and turns.

***

The next thing I knew I was in the apartment of some unfathomably rich girl from Brazil. She had a dorm room on campus, but she really lived in the Westin Hotel downtown.

I hadn't planned on coming to her party, yet somehow I found myself there.

The lights were off; the apartment was dark and the only illumination came from candles. There was fancy furniture, flowers in vases and real art on the walls. I couldn't help but contrast the apartment to my own dorm room.

In my room, where another person slept across from me, almost close enough to reach out and touch, I tacked an elephant tapestry to wall. It never seemed to stay up. There was an old floral couch that had been passed down to my roommate. The couch had been in many rooms before; many people I did not know had sat on it. People had probably even made love on that tattered couch.

I had a dingy little rug that covered the linoleum floor. We bought the rug for $60 at a sale outside of one of the freshmen dorms. It was dirt-colored, and I loved it for hiding the dust that gathered in that little room.

The crowd at this girl's apartment was made up of the young wealthy elite from New York, Europe and beyond; many of whom I individually liked, though at that moment I couldn't have cared less about any of them. They were all just standing around sipping wine talking about nothing. They were 20-years-old, and they all just wanted to act like they were 40.

I couldn't relate to such sentiments.

Why don't they get it? We have all of our lives to be old and bored.

The party was dull.

I want to dance! I want to rage!

Hell, I wanted to leave, but I was cheap, and I wasn't ready to pay for a cab home. Plus, there was so much free alcohol and food; there was no way I was going to leave so soon.

Scanning the room, I noticed there was a sushi platter on the counter. With my gaze focused upon the tuna rolls and sashimi, I began making my way over. Along the way, I sloppily greeted the people I knew; their eyes narrowed as they tried to understand my incoherent sentences before they dismissed me with condescending pats on the shoulder.

No one else was eating the sushi, so I figured it wouldn't be an issue if I really dug in. One piece after the other, I shoveled the room-temperature-raw-fish into my mouth.

The hostess made her way over.

"Hello," I said, giving her a kiss on both cheeks.

"Great party," I said, as I noticed how easy it was to detect the heavy slur that accompanied my speech. I felt my right eye going slightly lazy, as it always did when I overindulged.

She smiled politely, but I could sense her insincerity; I could tell she regretted inviting me.

But, in that moment, I truly didn't care.

Maybe I'll be embarrassed tomorrow, I thought. *But tomorrow feels so far away.*

Besides, I justified, *she's a girl who rarely drinks, and she's not known for being especially fun.*

If anything, I convinced myself, *she's reputed as being a bit of a drag.*

I'm the fun one.

The hostess not so discretely offered me water, and though I'd rather have had champagne, I chugged it because I was not actively trying to be disrespectful.

Popping another piece of sushi into my mouth, I surveyed the room.

Where is that boy?

As I didn't know what else one would do in such a situation of inaction, I grabbed a nearby bottle of Pinot Noir and poured myself a glass. I knew I probably didn't need it, but when had that ever stopped someone before?

I walked over to the bathroom and locked myself in. The bathroom was spotless and marble. There were plush rugs next to the tub, and beautiful fixtures; it was so much nicer than the bathrooms in the houses of even the most successful people from my childhood.

Though I didn't particularly like living in an open double room and having to fear that I was getting athletes foot or worse every time I showered in my dorm's public bathroom, there was something about the fanciness of this apartment that made me feel quite sad on behalf of the hostess.

She'll never have the chance to be young again.

I was of the belief that these were supposed to be the years of BYOB sushi restaurants and frat parties; of regrettable trysts and living off pizza and ramen noodles. This girl was leading a more extravagant life as a sophomore in college than I thought I would live as a 50-year-old man. She was paying thousands and thousands of dollars to live miles away from campus in an upscale chain hotel; she was paying thousands of dollars to be alone.

Even in the bathroom, the only light came from candles. I laughed thinking that someone probably came in and decorated this party for this girl; this party that then turned out to be a bit dull. The whole thing felt so gimmicky; she was acting like a Stepford Wife. Everything felt like such a charade.

The room suddenly felt too dark, so I turned the lights on. Then the brightness felt way too harsh on my eyes, so I immediately switched them back off.

I was tired of holding the glass of wine – it suddenly felt so heavy in my hands. I thought about leaving it on the counter, but I then decided that would be a total waste, so I chugged it instead. Filling the glass with tap water from the sink, I gulped that down too.

The whole time, I watched myself in the ornate mirror.

I moved closer to the perfectly cleaned glass.

Jesus, my pupils are huge.

Wooziness took over my body, and there was a strange pounding in my head. I wanted to go home – I needed to go home – but I bent my legs and decided to lie down on the floor for just a minute, instead.

***

"Ow!" I screamed, as I felt an incredibly sharp pain shoot up my spine.

I knew the pain; it came from being roughly penetrated.

My vision was blurry, but it was starting to refocus. I slowly realized that I was in my dorm room, sprawled on the carpet, completely naked. The overheard lights were off, but my roommate's desk lamp was on. I could make out a naked boy knelt between my spread legs.

"Ow!" I screamed again.

"You said you wanted to have sex!" the boy shouted.

I was taken aback by the boy's anger.

I stared at him like some alien specimen. Eventually, he sat back on his ankles, and I could see his erect penis was covered with a condom.

I was not scared.

In fact, I believed the boy; I was sure that I did tell him I wanted to have sex. I just didn't remember.

Pushing myself to think harder, I was able to piece together that this was the same boy from earlier. He was that same boy who had been with me the whole night. Though I forgot his name, I was impressed by his dedication.

Unfortunately for the boy, I felt rather queasy and having sex on the floor was the last thing I wanted to do.

"Can't we just cuddle?" I asked as I sat up and grabbed his leg, pulling him toward me.

My vision was progressively getting clearer, and though I was not feeling very attracted to the boy, my fear of loneliness outweighed my sexual standards.

Simply, I didn't want to be left alone.

"No," the boy aggressively responded. "What the fuck?"

In a rage, the boy jerked away and swiftly started gathering his clothes.

"But, I love you," I said as tears streamed down my face. I was trying so hard to remember his name.

"You're being fucking crazy," he shouted.

The boy got dressed; then he made his way toward the door.

Gathering my strength, I managed to stand up and walk over to the bed. I was still crying, but I wasn't even sad. I was just so tired and confused.

I lay in my bed and curled up into a ball. Pulling the covers over my head, I hoped that being in a homemade cocoon would make the world stop spinning so fast.

What is this boy's name? I asked myself. *Wait, why do I even care? He's an asshole.*

Anger washed over me, and I threw the covers off of my head. I sat up and looked for something to throw at the boy; something hard; something that would hurt.

I wanted to shout at the boy; I want to scream something mean he would never forget. I needed to have the last word. I wanted to make the boy felt bad for leaving, even though I really didn't want him to stay.

I couldn't muster up the energy to do it. Instead, I curled back into fetal position and drifted away.

{ 24 }

Rolling

"Ok, on the count of three we'll all take it," someone shouted from the center of the group.

I looked around the room, at the thirty plus members of my friend group who were packed into this space. We called this room the 'Stripper Pole Lounge,' as Brown's 'Poler Bears' had set up two poles for practice. Normally, the room was locked, but that night we found our way in.

Everyone milled about anxiously. Between our fingers we pinched blue pills shaped like stars.

Ecstasy.

"Alright, one, two three, NOW," the voice yelled.

Everyone swallowed their pills.

This moment reminded me of Jonestown. How easy would it be to fall into a cult looking for answers? How easy would it be to join such a group in hopes it might make you feel whole?

Now, we waited.

We waited for the pills to hit our stomach. We waited for the chemicals to spread. We waited to feel fucked up. We waited to feel alive.

I'd earlier read what happens to your body when one took Ecstasy. Yet, the details were immediately lost on me. I knew there was something about neurotransmitters, and the drug affecting the reuptake of serotonin. Dopamine was also involved, though I couldn't remember exactly how.

What I did know was the way I soon would feel.

I knew that momentarily I would feel lightheaded and super-sensory all at once; I'd be utterly stimulated and yet I'd be coasting in a dreamlike trance.

"Let's go!" someone shouted. We spilled out of the room and then out of the dormitory like ants from their hill. We poured onto the street and fought our way into the line of cabs.

"Wait," my friends said, grabbing my shoulder. "How do you feel?"

"Good," I said dreamily. "You?"

"I haven't taken it yet," she said.

"Why?"

"I couldn't stop picturing tomorrow's paper having the headline '40 Brown Students Drop Dead from Bad Ecstasy,'" she grimly confessed.

My eyes widened. The thought had never even crossed my mind.

"But, it sounds like that won't be the case," she said, reassuring both herself and me.

***

Later that night, at the Girl Talk concert, we congregated in a sea of hundreds of Brown students.

The lights were beautiful, and I felt like I had senses beyond synesthesia; it was as though I could feel the sound of the music. From the stage, toilet paper was dispensed through the air, and it gracefully descended upon us. Water drops hit us in the face.

It was ethereal.

It was as if the experience was made for those of us who were rolling.

These were the moments I felt most religious; the moments I felt most pulled away from my sense of grounded self.

Someone grabbed my hand; it was a girl with whom I was a casual friend, though not that close.

She stared at me; her eyes locked into mine.

Her pupils are so large.

She took my hand in hers, and she squeezed, hard. Her hands felt icy. I thought it must feel like holding the hand of a corpse.

"I'm so glad we're friends," she said, squeezing again while maniacally smiling.

"Me too," I said, forcing myself to seem cheery, though her face was creeping me out.

It wasn't that I disliked her, it was just that I was able to tell it was the drugs speaking, not her.

On any other afternoon, this interaction never would have taken place.

And she was not the first person to do this; I'd already had three similar exchanges, with almost the exact lines.

Why is it that we only allow ourselves to be vulnerable when we are fucked up? And if we are fucked up, then are we really being vulnerable, at all?

She said something else I couldn't hear but pretended to, and I kissed her cheek.

Maybe she will move on.

She seemed satisfied. We let go of each other's hands, and I watched her walk to another boy two people away from me.

She tapped his shoulder in the exact same way she'd just tapped mine.

He turned, they locked eyes, and she took his hands in hers.

{ 25 }

Faux-Vulnerability

As I sat on the bed with my friend's girlfriend after a long night out, I wanted to tell her everything I'd never told a soul.

We weren't that close, but in that moment, the many drinks I'd had made me want to talk; I couldn't keep my lips sealed; I needed to let out my secrets.

"I don't think I'm lovable," I blurted out.

"What?" she asked, taken aback.

"I don't think I'll ever find someone who loves me," I said. "I think I'm just too complicated."

"Seamus, that's not true."

"It is," I said. "I think I'm okay with it."

"Everyone is lovable," she said. "A lot of people love you."

"No," I said. "I don't think I'll ever find anyone who is in love with me."

A single tear slid down my cheek.

She put her hand on my arm.

"You will," she said.

"I'm not ever sad about it," I said, sniffling. "I'm not even sure why I'm crying."

***

The next morning, my friend asked me about the conversation.

"It was nice," I said, struggling to recall everything that was said. "I think we bonded."

"Seamus, I don't want to be mean," said my friend. "But, whatever you said, you really freaked her out."

"What?" I asked, surprised. "I was just complaining about dating."

"That's not what she said," continued my friend. "She said you were being really dark. She said your eyes glazed over with darkness."

{ 26 }

Away

"I've decided I'm going to go study abroad in India," I told my dad toward the end of my sophomore year, as we walked our dog around the reservoir. I was home for the weekend, and spring was turning to summer, and a warm breeze was rolling up the hill.

"Why India?" he asked.

"I don't want to go to Europe like everyone else," I said. "Plus, this program is six months instead of three."

"Okay," he said. "But, do you have a reason to go besides wanting to do something that's not the same from your friends?"

"I just think it will be really nice to change my way of life for awhile," I said, not understanding why he wasn't automatically excited for me. "Plus, for the program, we'll be in the Himalayas and then in Delhi. It will be impossible to party as much as I'm partying now…it will be a good break."

"I'm glad to hear you want a break," he said. "But, I just want to make sure you aren't taking an extreme measure simply to be extreme."

Of course I knew there was a part of me that wanted to prove I could live in a country so different from the USA, like India, on my own for six months. I was aware that I did feel a smug satisfaction in thinking that I was going away for so much longer than my friends while also choosing to live in a place that would be so much less comfortable.

"I'm not," I said. "I can just tell this is the perfect for me."

"I'm not saying I disapprove," he said. "I'm just saying you should think…"

"I'm going," I interrupted. "I already told Brown I'm going."

{ 27 }

Xanax & India

Withdrawal is never good; withdrawal is especially detestable when it's medically unsupervised in a foreign country. This was a lesson that I had to learn the hard way when I found myself feeling like Alice in Wonderland after she eats the cake marked "Eat Me" and suddenly becomes a disproportionate giant; monstrous yet fragile.

It was one of those days with an overcast gray sky and thick sitting air; the way Hollywood always portrays 1970's San Francisco. Rickshaws sped past and cows roamed the road. It was a mere 24 hours after I decided that I was going to take matters into my own hands and end my Xanax addiction.

I was already feeling the intense side effects of withdrawal. I was lightheaded and wobbly. Though there was no breeze, I felt unsteady, like I was swaying. My sensations of derealization were so intense that I felt as though I was levitating a foot above the hectic New Delhi street.

I began to convulsively gasp; I was drowning in the air in which everyone else seemed to be breathing just fine. As the scenes of my imminent death flashed in my head, I stumbled – slamming my sandal-clad foot perfectly into a glob of cow manure. I started to fold, and my vision went out of focus.

My American friend, Tyler, who had been around for the entirety of my anti-anxiety medication "over-indulgence," grabbed me by the wrist and dragged me the few blocks to the local cabstand. In broken Hindi, she somehow managed to communicate to the driver that we needed to quickly be delivered to the nearest hospital.

While this specific withdrawal-induced panic attack was just another episode of my four-month mental unraveling, it wasn't until I was being wheeled into the quaint, if not terribly outdated, Indian hospital that I realized how absolutely insane I not only looked, but had become. From my loosely fitting white-boy-in-India linen shirt and culturally-inappropriate-above-the-knee shorts, to my cow-shit strewn foot; from my sunken, absent eyes to my emaciated limbs; I had become the poster child of dysfunction.

I was promptly brought into a room with stiff cots separated by retractable curtains. The nurses wasted no time in closing the curtains around me as to not disturb the other patients and their families.

I was in a sheer panic; I shook uncontrollably and my vision was blocked by the endless refills from my tear ducts. I compulsively moved two fingers back and forth from my neck to my chest as I searched for a heartbeat. My subconscious paranoia had taken over; I could feel no pulse. I pleaded for the doctors to save me. I was convinced that my heart was going to quit at any second.

Those feelings were nothing new; I had spent every night for months trying to coax myself to sleep while battling that sinking feeling that never failed to consume my mind. I was utterly certain every night that *this* would be the night that my heart would finally stop pumping blood through my veins. I was always positive that *this* headache was actually an aneurysm ready to burst. All of these nights ended the same: After taking a few Xanax and chasing them with watered-down whiskey, I would finally be able to subdue this fear of never waking up enough to finally drift into sedative-induced stupor.

Despite my familiarity with these psychosomatic symptoms of anxiety attacks, the degree to which they were hitting me in the hospital was incomparable to my prior experiences. The unfamiliarity of the hospital wasn't helping. Unlike in America, where every medical supply seemed to be readily available to the hospital staff, I was disturbed to discover that at this Indian hospital, the doctor gave the patient's companion a list so that she could purchase each item – whether it was a pill, a needle, or an IV bag – a la carte from a desk in the lobby. Not only did this transaction involve overcoming a language barrier, it also meant standing in a long, slow-moving line.

Tyler had to continuously go back and forth from my bed to the desk to get my medical supplies. When you're having an anti-anxiety-medication-addiction-withdrawal-induced-panic attack at a less-than-modern hospital in New Delhi, the last thing I wanted was to be left alone. I worked myself into such hysteria that I vomited the remnants of my McSpicy Paneer, which I had foolishly consumed as a home-away-from-home comfort food a few hours earlier.

I fell onto on my stomach with my head over the side of the bed retching into a bucket – all the while pleading both aloud and in my head for salvation. Cold hands pressed themselves against my lower back as my shorts and underwear were swiftly pulled down to my knees, leaving my butt completely exposed. In complete confusion I craned my neck to look at the nurse whose minimal spoken English abilities did not prevent me from knowing – from the locking of our eyes – that something painful was on its way.

"Breathe," she said firmly as she jabbed what felt like the longest and thickest needle known to man into my semi-clenched behind. After the initial jolt of pain shot through my body, I began to feel an instantaneous sense of relief. She continued her work; shoving a cocktail of pills into my mouth while inserting an IV into my arm.

I looked up and tried to catch the nurse's attention. I was still gently sobbing with streaks of throw-up smeared across my cheeks. When I caught her eye, I managed to whimper, "Am I going to die?" The nurse shook her head and giggled as she pushed her cart away.

The injection of what must have been Librium set in, and I began feeling woozy as my sense of imminent tragedy subsided. I silently sat up and peeked around the curtain. From my little area I was able to see a stoic younger woman hunched over the bed of an unconscious man. From the way her trembling fingers were entwined with his, it was clear that he was her husband; I could feel how much she loved him. His face was smashed; it was covered in blood, and he lay nearly lifeless, yet somehow still breathing.

At the bed next to them were three adult-children gathered around an old man with an oxygen mask. He looked very much on his way out of this life, and they held onto each other as they came to terms with his impending passage.

Tacked directly on the wall between their two beds was the calendar sold by Palna, the orphanage where I volunteered. Palna means, "cradle," in Hindi, and the name was not random: A cradle was installed within the secure wall that surrounded the facility. Parents could anonymously drop their babies and small children off in the cradle – which was manned by security guards – when they could no longer provide for them.

For the month of November, the calendar showcased the grinning face of Shivani, one of the children I spent time with during my visits. I pictured Shivani, shrieking in delight as she played hide and seek in the open courtyards of the orphanage. She was mischievous, and sneakily pinched the other kids when she thought none of the adults were watching.

Utter chaos was occurring around me as patients and doctors zoomed in and out of the emergency room, but I fixed my stare upon Shivani's two-dimensional smirk. I thought about the two patients and their families.

These are people with real problems, I thought to myself. *What is wrong with me?*

***

Two months before, in September, my dad had come to visit.

Waking up early, I took the metro to meet him at the New Delhi airport. A gate at the High Court of Delhi had been bombed the week before, and I had stopped taking the metro as the line I took passed right beneath the site.

With my newfound constant fear of dying, I couldn't handle being on the crowded metro cars. I couldn't bring myself to be packed in a space where every inch was filled with humans, though months earlier I'd been unfazed.

Instead, I found myself spending increasing amounts of time inside. The world felt scary; too overwhelming. It was a fear so intense I had never experienced before.

On this morning, I convinced myself that the metro was the most practical way to travel. I had always been adventurous, fearless. I had never been afraid of death, and now I needed to work up the courage to just ride the metro.

My dad's visit coincided with my first (unsuccessful) Xanax detox, and as I sat on the train an old man with a traditional sword sat across from me. I spent the next half hour of my journey thinking about all of the terrible ways my life could end from that cool metal sliding into my essential organs before being swiftly pulled out.

I completely lost it the second I met my dad at the gate of the uncharacteristically calm airport. He came off the plane beaming; he was so excited to be in India for the first time.

I began instantly weeping, and continued to do so for the entirety of the first two days of his visit. I confessed my feelings of anxiety and dependence upon Xanax. I tried weaning myself off of Xanax with his support, but his presence could not stop the withdrawal effects. I had constant headaches and debilitating waves of panic; my appetite disappeared and the tears just wouldn't stop.

***

On the third night of my dad's visit, we went for a walk in a beautifully preserved ancient garden. We watched the sunset as we sat on top of a structure that had occupied that space since the days of the Mughal Empire. I could not relax in the slightest or even notice the natural painting that lay before me. I sat in an auto-rickshaw with him and sobbed like I had not sobbed since I was a child.

He asked me why I had come to India, especially for six months.

"To try to fight inequality," I bullshitted.

"How?" he asked.

I could not provide him with even the simplest of answers; I honestly did not know.

"You came to run away from yourself," he told me. "And I think you're learning the hard way, that whatever you're running away from will always catch up with you."

He told me that the most glaring indicator of someone being mentally unwell is their complete self-centeredness and inability to speak about anything beyond themselves; for that entire week all I could talk or think about was how miserable I felt.

I remembered years before, in high school, when my dad joked about the glaring disconnect between my party boy behaviors and my quest to be valedictorian. "You have the most imbalanced existence of anyone I've ever met," he said.

And there I was, years later, an Ivy League student abroad who had decided to come to India to pursue interests of social justice, but was instead spending his days drinking whiskey, taking Xanax and crying.

I realized that he was right.

**

As I sprawled in the hospital bed, having a teen-celebrity-style-substance-abuse-induced-breakdown in a windowless room. I tried to recount exactly how I had gotten to this point. I had always had a susceptibility to overwhelming anxiety and a tendency for self-medication, but never would I have imagined myself having to be sedated through an injection because I was so terribly certain that I was on the brink of untimely death.

Over and over, I used the same piece of aging prescription paper to refill my stash. The pharmacies were from a different time, entering one felt like being transported back 50 years. Never in the US would I have gotten away with this method.

The first bottle of "take as needed" pills was only supposed to last a few weeks, but I had been taking quadruple dosages for months. I jokingly referred to the small change pocket of my wallet where I kept my Xanax as the "Land of Naughtiness;" it was an attempt to deflect attention from a glaring addiction.

I'll take Valium to detox from Xanax, I convinced myself.

Becoming overconfident, I had tried to write myself a prescription for Valium on a piece of loose-leaf paper. When I took it to the chemist, the old man behind the counter had narrowed his eyes as he shook his head at my pathetic attempt. "No!" he said, wagging his finger in my face. I snatched the paper from his hand and left in a huff.

During my dad's stay, I weaned myself off the medication, but within a week or two of his leaving I relapsed. The whole experience shook my entire perception of an addict's mentality. I was not in denial of being addicted to Xanax; in fact I was completely aware. I had reached a point where I believed I did not know how else to survive during my time in India.

I must attempt to make the addiction as functional as possible until I can return home, I told myself. *When I'm home I'll have access to an abundance of readily available psychotherapists and psychiatrists who can fix me.*

I never thought to ask myself why I was so broken.

***

The addiction had all begun in the most unsuspecting of ways. After spending a day shopping, my friends and I decided to have dinner in some nondescript, poorly lit, overpriced chain restaurant in an upscale Indian mall.

Midway through the meal I had a strange headache and kept losing focus; I had the terrifying sensation that my time to die was imminent. As I sat at the table and tried to continue the conversation, I kept having that same feeling as when you're on the verge of sleep and you suddenly feel a sharp jolt of free fall until you crash back into reality.

I excused myself to go the bathroom, and started pacing in the corridor of the mall.

I can't die outside of Gucci.

In retrospect, I had been on a massive alcohol bender, and this feeling was my first experience with withdrawal symptoms. But, at the time, all I could comprehend was that I felt like I was dying.

I finally told the others what I felt and one friend explained that I was having a panic attack, which she had suffered aplenty after experiencing a traumatic loss. "Just keep taking deep breaths and I'll give you a Xanax when we get home," she offered. I managed to get through the next hour by cycling deep breaths and drinking cold water. Once we got home, she slipped me the pill that I quickly popped in my mouth.

Within twenty minutes I felt calm and grounded. I was no longer afraid that I would perish at any moment. Frankly, I felt happy, and realized I had not felt much but despair in many weeks. I felt a relief I had missed.

And so it began.

***

When the terrifying panic attacks - and what seemed to be a permanent tension headache - kept coming back over the next couple of days after the mall experience, I went to see the University-recommended physician. After a few moments of speaking with her, she quickly wrote me a prescription for Xanax and sent me on my way. Unfortunately, she failed to mention any addictive side effects of the prescription drug, or its dangerous interactions with alcohol.

Blissful in my ignorance – and functionally sedated – I continued the school-boy-by-day-party-boy-by-night lifestyle that my friends and I had fallen into. But everything became much more intense. I blacked out multiple nights a week. It was not blacking out, like I did at Brown, where I had splotches of memory. When I drank alcohol with Xanax, it was full-blown unconsciousness; I was 'roofying' myself.

I would wake up the morning with literally no recollection of the previous night. I didn't care. I dissolved Xanax in my beer, and popped it recreationally as I took shots at clubs.

I had to be filled in about my outlandish behaviors; I lost a shoe at brunch when I blacked out at 2 pm; I woke up under my bed; I lost multiple wallets and cameras; I cried about being financially stressed as I spent hundreds of dollars on wine in a single night at the most expensive bar in the city; I had to be carried into my apartment by a driver who was employed by my friend; like a corpse, he slung me over his shoulder as he hauled my limp body up the stairs.

Even on nights that we didn't go out, my routine was seriously affected by my medication and alcohol intake. I was anxious all of the time. I couldn't fall asleep unless I took increasingly higher doses of Xanax.

I felt nauseous every time I ate. I began taking Xanax multiple times a day; I wanted to ensure the calm mental wave carried me from the moment I woke up until the moment I fell asleep.

My moods gradually became less varied. I was no longer anxious, but I was also never especially happy or sad; I was unexpressive and blank. I felt detached from the people I loved; I was emotionally cold in a way that I never knew was possible.

One day, I sat on a speeding auto-rickshaw – an open-air golf cart-like vehicle – on the way to meet my friends. As the driver recklessly wove through heavy traffic, I observed the scenery and life of the Indian streets. It felt like a movie I was watching more than my reality. I felt so far removed from my "real" life, as though I were in some dream that wouldn't seem to end.

***

As I lay in that hospital bed, I felt like the world's biggest hypocrite for all of the times I had made fun of Lindsay Lohan's "exhaustion" hospitalizations. Powering through the stifling post-sob headache that brought me back to childhood tantrums after being grounded from TV, I searched my bed for my wallet. I found it near the edge of the bed, where it had fallen out of my pocket. I picked it up and opened the "Land of Naughtiness."

I counted my pills. 15. Just enough to make it through the last couple of days before I would finally board my plane to take me home.

I'll stop taking Xanax then, I told myself, as I swallowed one of the small white tablets and allowed myself to drift away.

{ 28 }

The Face

I lay on the couch in the cavernous living room of the Victorian house one of my best friends, Jonny, had wrangled for us to live in that spring at Brown.

The downstairs of the house was mostly empty of furniture, except for an old card table in the dining room and a few scattered couches in the double living room. The house always reminded me of the ornate and hollow mansion from *Garden State*.

Across from the couch where I lied, a humungous painting hung on the wall, while professional DJ equipment that Jonny had movers bring blasted music.

People danced around the room, it was one of our first nights back at Brown after almost half of us had returned from our study abroad programs.

I knew I should be greeting people, as I was one of the hosts of the party, but being social felt overwhelming.

A few of us had taken mushrooms and washed them down with prosecco from Jonny's fancy champagne flutes.

The shrooms were kicking in, and I'd found two familiar friends and latched onto them; in my head I decided they were the only people I felt comfortable speaking to.

"Seamus, hi!" a girl exclaimed as she made her way over.

"I'm so sorry, I can't talk right now," I said covering my face and giggling.

"He's tripping," said one of the friends who I'd designated a protector.

It felt so nice to be back at Brown. It was freezing outside the house, but our living room felt warm. It was nice to see all of these people I hadn't seen in seven months, even if I couldn't handle talking to them right now.

Under a psychiatrist's supervision, I'd weaned myself off Xanax while simultaneously beginning to take Zoloft to treat my anxiety.

I felt like such a happier human.

Xanax was out of my life, and I'd convinced myself that had been the problem substance.

Alcohol and other drugs were still fair game.

"Seamus!" I heard a voice say, as I rolled to hide my face.

"He's tripping right now," said my friend.

When I heard the other person walk away, I sat up and stared at the painting on the wall.

"I see a face in the painting," I said. "Right there in the center."

"There isn't a face," my friend said, while giggling and glancing at our third friend.

"I see a face," I said, convinced. "I'd never seen it before, but I can't stop seeing it now."

{ 29 }

Breaking Point

It started with the creation of a potent cocktail in a large movie theater cup. The cocktail's recipe was simple: Pour iced tea, vodka and gin into the cup until the liquid mixture nearly reached the brim.

I sipped from the cup and then I gulped; I offered it up to other people.

Some let a few drops pour into their mouths.

"That's disgusting," my friend said. "It literally tastes like rubbing alcohol."

But I knew how it worked with nasty drinks: The more you consumed, the less you tasted.

The drink took me on a journey.

A curtain closed over my eyes, and every so often it would open. I had no control.

One moment, I was on the Main Green of Brown's campus. It was 4/20 – the unofficial holiday of marijuana consumption – and everyone was smoking. People smoked from joints, bowls, blunts and vaporizers. The air was literally filled with smoke.

I blinked, and there was calmness; I recognized I was moving, breathing and living, though I was not aware or in control of my actions.

When I came back to myself, I was at a long table at a restaurant with a group of friends.

We ate tarmasalata and shared pitchers of sangria. We clinked our cups together and talked about the Spring Weekend concert and the after parties that were happening that night.

I kept drinking, and my mind retreated to that place of unconscious functioning, what is commonly called a 'brownout.'

Suddenly, I was home in my living room. A group was gathered around me, and people were drinking heavily; the concert was soon.

I did lines of coke. In between lines, I took shots of chilled vodka. I stuffed pocket shots of whiskey into my underwear, so I could bring them into the concert.

I thought I was slipping back into the brownout, but I fell deeper down the rabbit hole.

I didn't come out.

I was gone. There was only blackness.

***

I woke up thrashing violently. I was kicking at the nurses and screaming at them to not touch me.

A man held me down, and all I could do was hurl insults and threats.

"I'll sue you!" I screamed. "Get the fuck off me!"

I'd never felt so insane. The more I kicked the harder he held me down. I felt so trapped, like an animal that had been caught and was about to be slaughtered. I knew the man would probably let me go if I stopped fighting, but I was scared he would still hold me down. So, I kept screaming and wriggling. I didn't want to lose.

"Seamus, calm down," I heard Jonny say, gripping my arm. "Calm down, or they're never going to let us leave."

I stopped moving.

I gasped for air.

As soon as I stopped screaming, I started sobbing. I didn't stop until I fell asleep.

***

When I woke again, I was speaking to Jonny.

My mouth was fully moving, and sentences were coming out, but I had no control of what I was saying; I had no memory of what I had already said.

I listened to my own voice.

"I hate myself," I cried. "I want to die."

"Seamus, seriously, just calm down," Jonny said. "You're just drunk."

"No, I'm not," I pleaded. "I hate my life and I think about killing myself all the time."

"You seemed perfectly happy before all of this," he said.

"I'm miserable!"

"Are you serious?" he asked.

I wasn't sure. I couldn't tell if the alcohol was creating false memories, or if it was exposing my subconscious thoughts. I wasn't sure if I was speaking my repressed truth, or lying through my teeth.

{ 30 }

Stop

"Hey, I need to talk to you," one of my roommates said as we walked home from class.

"Okay," I replied, suspicious of what she wanted to discuss.

It was a sunny spring day, and we were walking past one of the lawns on Brown's campus; we were less than a block away from our house.

"Want to sit here?" she asked

"Sure," I said, feeling a strange impulse to run.

We sat down, facing each other.

Instantly, I could tell the conversation was going to be awkward. I kept averting my gaze.

My roommate stared off into the distance.

The silence lingered; my stomach rose and then fell.

I hated being confronted, and I couldn't imagine what else the conversation might be.

Suddenly, she moved and looked at me.

"Okay, I'm just going to say it," she said.

I nodded.

"When you were hospitalized, you said you would stop drinking," she said. "You only waited three weeks before starting again."

"I'm fine," I said calmly.

"I can't watch you drink," she said. "You just shouldn't be drinking."

I tensed up; I was already feeling defensive.

"We've all been talking about it as roommates," she said. "I talked to my mom about it this morning, and she said maybe we should call your parents."

I felt so betrayed. The thought of people having conversations about this behind my back made me feel physically ill.

"I just can't believe you would even consider that before trying to talk to me first," I said coldly.

"Well, that's why I didn't," she said, clearly caught off guard by me going on the offense. "And I'm not threatening you, but if you keep drinking we might have to."

"I won't drink then," I said flatly.

"Are you mad at me?" she said.

"No," I lied. "I'm not mad, I'm just overwhelmed."

"I'm just doing this because I love you," she said.

That wasn't what it felt like to me; I felt attacked. My drinking was a part of my personality, so by attacking my drinking, I felt like she was attacking me.

Inside my head, I was thinking of all of the ways I could be mean to her, all of her behaviors I could criticize. I wanted to get even.

I felt blindsided.

"So you'll stop drinking?" she asked.

"Yes," I said. "I'll stop."

"Are you sure you aren't angry?"

"I'm not," I said. "I just want to be alone."

"Okay," she said. "Well, let me know if you want to talk. I want to support you."

"Okay," I said. "Thanks."

She leaned in to give me a hug, and I half-heartedly hugged her back.

She got up quickly, and walked away. I wanted her to go, but I didn't want to be alone; I didn't know how to be alone.

As soon as she was out of sight, I turned my head and cried.

The tears came from anger. I was angry with my roommate for confronting me, but I was angrier with myself for needing to be confronted.

I knew she was right, but I didn't want her to be; I was out of control, and didn't know how to reel myself in.

{ 31 }

A Break

I spent the summer "sober" between my junior and senior years in New York.

But, my sobriety came with a fine print, and personal touches.

"I said I wouldn't drink, I never said I wouldn't do drugs," I told my friend as she narrowed her eyes at the idea of giving me the pill of Ecstasy she had just found in her purse.

"Okay," she said. "Are you sure though?"

"Yes," I told her. "It's fine, it's not like I had a problem with Ecstasy."

I almost told her that I'd rolled on Ecstasy three times during the last week of school, when I'd already *technically* been in this period of abstaining from alcohol.

I realized that sharing that information might not exactly help my case.

She handed me the pill.

"It's from a year ago, though," she said. "I can't promise it will still be good."

***

I took that pill as we drove to The Box, a nightclub that had turn-of-the-century-style sex shows.

Jonny bought a table that overlooked the stage with his parents' credit card.

There was a big a group of us, and the cocktail waitresses delivered magnum bottles of expensive liquor to our table.

Everyone grew drunker and drunker, as my Ecstasy began to set in.

I flirted with a sweet boy I had a crush on named Sam, who also went to Brown and had grown up in the same Upper East Side wealthy finance world as Jonny.

Sam was kind and self-assured. I felt calm around him. He was one of the first boys I could actually imagine myself dating.

I wanted that to happen, badly.

We talked the whole night, as we always did, but then at the end he left the club to go see another boy.

"Are you sad?" asked Jonny.

"No," I said as I optimistically floated on the Ecstasy's sweet release. "It will happen, I know it will. It will happen in time."

***

The wheels lifted and I looked out the window of the small plane. Sam's parents chartered the flight to take us to their house on Martha's Vineyard for the weekend.

We took a car to the airport in Teterboro, New Jersey where we pranced onto the plane with practically no security. The whole experience felt so surreal.

As the plane rose higher into the sky, I thought about how easy it would be for the plane to plummet; I wasn't even sure that I'd be that surprised if it did; I almost was more prepared to crash than to not, it all felt so foreign.

Everyone else was drinking rosé, but I was determined to keep my promise to people that I'd take the summer off from alcohol after the most recent hospitalization. I explored the drawer below my seat and selected a bag of chips, instead.

I opened the bag, but I didn't eat the chips. I pushed the bag aside, instead.

I thought back to when I was younger, and any plane ride would have been a treat. Here I was now, on a private flight, speeding toward an island where I'd never been.

How could I tell my friends from home or my family about this without sounding obnoxious?

I felt so caught between two worlds.

Class is a strange thing; so glaringly subtle in its hierarchy. What the rich do, what they have, is what we are taught we should aspire to achieve. Yet, when we are able to experience those lavish things, it's somehow tacky to disclose that we enjoyed it; that it made us feel special.

I was on a private plane, flying to an island I'd grown up only hearing about, and I was uncomfortable admitting to myself that I was blown away by such luxury.

So, I didn't; I pretended six twenty-somethings jetting away from the City was normal, something you might see all the time.

The thing was, for my friends, it was normal, though, for me, it was not.

It was a difference I thought only I noticed; it was a difference I thought only I felt.

**

"Why are you only friends with rich people?" a newer friend asked me that summer.

"I'm not," I fired back, pissed.

I began listing my friends who weren't rich.

"It just so happens that most of my friends who can afford to live in New York for the summer and barely be paid are already well-off," I concluded.

A moment passed.

"Well, and you have a crush on Sam, who is also super wealthy," he said.

"That has nothing to do with why I like him. Should I not like him just because we're from different class backgrounds?" I said, meaning it. "Plus, you're trying to be friends with all of my friends anyways, so why are you criticizing me?"

Why the fuck does it matter to you? I wanted to ask him, angrily.

But, I didn't. It felt cruel to press him further in an argument that I knew I would win.

It's a dynamic that was not unfamiliar: We were two people who felt lower on the class hierarchy. Instead of coming together, we wanted to tear each other apart.

I was aware of these undertones, but I still wanted to do it; he had made me feel shitty, and I wanted him to feel the same way.

Why?

***

I arrived to lunch with a free spirited girl from Brown.

She beat me to the small Mexican restaurant in SoHo.

When I walked down the stairs into the basement level dining room, I immediately noticed the pitcher sitting on the table.

"I ordered us a pitcher of margaritas!" she exclaimed.

Shit, I thought. *She doesn't know I'm not drinking.*

I could have told her; I so easily could have told her.

But, if she didn't know I wasn't supposed to be drinking, then she wouldn't think it was a big deal if I did.

It will just be this once, I told myself. *I'll be able to see how I respond to alcohol; I'll be able to test if I'm ready to drink again.*

But, what if she does tell people? I pondered. *Deny until I die, I suppose.*

I sat down, and smiled; I thought about it one last time.

It was so hot outside and the drops of the condensation slid down the pitcher's side.

The drops were beautiful; the drink called to me.

I reached out and grabbed the pitcher.

I poured myself a glass.

I drank.

***

The summer had passed, and Sam and I had grown much closer.

My feelings toward him were no secret, though still nothing had happened between us.

"I've been thinking about drinking when we go back to school," I told him at brunch, one of the last days of summer.

"I don't think you should," he said, looking up and nervously smiling. "You seem so much happier now."

{ 33 }

The Beginning of the End

It's been almost three months since that hospitalization, I thought to myself staring at the bottle of rosé and picturing what it might be like to just have one glass. *I should be fine to drink again. I've done my time and I'm allowed to have fun like everyone else. I shouldn't punish myself forever.*

I was in the Hampton's staying with my friend from Brown. Her neighbors were having a sprawling annual party. Lanterns hung from the trees, hundreds of people gathered to drink and whirl around the dance floor. It was decadent, and whimsical.

I wanted to be drunk like everyone else.

I knew I could sneak alcohol, but that felt so juvenile. I wanted to just drink normally; I wanted to be a normal drinker.

"I think I might have a glass of wine," I told my friend.

"Are you sure?" she asked.

"Yes," I said. "I've been thinking about it, and I want to try healthily drinking again."

"Okay," she said shrugging, both distracted and slightly drunk herself.

I started drinking the rosé.

It tasted so sweet and crisp. After having so many nights apart from alcohol, I felt gleeful to be reunited.

I was careful not to overindulge; I was so much more aware than I had been in the past.

Of course, one glass still turned to two, and then three glasses into four.

The night felt magical, as I slowly became drunk for the first time in months.

When I looked up I saw Bill and Hillary Clinton waltz around the dance floor.

What the fuck is my life? I thought, smiling to myself, and taking a sip of my drink.

{ 34 }

Liquid Courage

After spending a sober summer too cautious to make a move, Sam I were finally intimate the second night of school.

With alcohol, I was confident and bold; I felt sexual and attractive.

I was not fearful.

Over the summer, when I had been sober, I thought I would be humiliated and devastated if I tried to kiss Sam and he rejected me.

I would have been so vulnerable; he would have known my mind was fully intact and I was well aware of what I was doing.

But, now alcohol provided the ultimate safety net. If Sam rejected my advance, I could just blame my attempt on being drunk.

Alcohol was not only the ultimate shield; it was also the most powerful emotional lubricant.

Alcohol allowed Sam and I to transcend friendship, to climb into bed.

Sobriety was not for me, I thought. *Being drunk helps me get what I want. Alcohol helps me achieve my dreams.*

{ 35 }

The Man in the Chair

I was afraid of intimacy.

That didn't mean, I was never intimate, it just meant I almost always drank heavily before I went to bed with another person.

Normally, I couldn't easily climax from the touch of another man. No matter the stimulation, oftentimes during sex or fooling around, I did not finish.

Was it shame? Was it a physical disorder?

I didn't know, but I was convinced it might be why I hadn't yet had a real relationship.

It was my senior year and I felt fully ready to confront the issue; I felt fully ready to finally have a boyfriend.

I was in love with Sam, I knew that, and when even his touch could not bring me to climax, I knew there was a serious problem.

This is not about me being uncomfortable with strangers; it is about me being uncomfortable with myself.

The woman at psych services referred me to a man named George who had an office in a trendy part of Providence.

I went to the office, and saw a man of fifty, quite unremarkable.

"I need help becoming comfortable with sex," I told him.

"Do you have sex?"

"Yes," I said. "Fairly often. I've just never enjoyed it."

He began only asking me questions about my alcohol and drug use.

How often do you drink?

Are there days you don't drink?

Have you ever been hospitalized?

Every word I said he seemed to be jotting down.

"Wow, you require a lot of paper," he said after only five minutes.

Not knowing how to respond, and feeling very confused about the direction in which the session was headed, I said nothing.

He didn't skip a beat.

What drugs do you?

Are you depressed?

How do you deal with your depression?

Do you drink when you're depressed?

"You know," he said, "Usually I would wait until the second session to say this, but you're an alcoholic."

I was shocked.

"What," I asked, my face burning with rage.

"Yup, now I know why they sent you here," he said.

I looked down at the card he had given me at the beginning of the session and at the bottom in bold letters was written **ADDICTION SPECIALIST**.

Suddenly, I understood. George thought that Brown had tried to trick me into going to an addiction specialist.

They wouldn't have, I thought.

Then I remembered the hospitalization in the spring; I recalled the concerned way the doctors at Brown's health services had looked at me when I went in for my follow up appointment.

Could I have been tricked?

"I'm not here to talk about drinking," I said. "I'm here to learn how to enjoy sex."

"It's all related," he said.

"I guess I don't see how."

"That's what we'll work on together," he said. "But, between now and the next session do you promise you won't drink?"

"Okay," I said.

"When should we next meet?" he asked.

"I'll call you to make the appointment," I said. "I'm still figuring out my schedule."

"Please do," he said, firmly. "I'm quite worried about you."

You don't even know me, I thought.

"I will," I said with a forced calmness.

I carefully stood up and made my way out of the door.

"It was nice to meet you," he said, sticking out his hand.

"You too," I said, making minimal eye contact.

In the hall, outside of his door, I crumpled up the business card he had given me and left it on the ground.

How dare he call me an alcoholic? I hissed to myself.

I hoped he saw the card on the ground and knew I would not be calling. I hoped he saw the card and felt bad for calling me an alcoholic, for offending me, a person who had simply come to him for help.

{ 35 }

Love

I had gotten what I wanted: A boyfriend, love and intimacy.

I was with Sam at a warm restaurant on a cold winter night; we held hands across the table.

I wasn't used to this. I wasn't used to public displays of affection that weren't drunken dance floor 'make outs.' I had truly believed I would never have a moment that so closely resembled the beautiful couples from movies.

In that moment, everything felt so right.

"I just have to tell you," the waitress said when she came back with our drinks. "You two are perfect together."

Usually, I agreed. Sometimes I felt like being with Sam – my first boyfriend – had finally made me feel whole; it had convinced me that I was lovable. With Sam, I had overcome my issues with intimacy. I was slowly growing comfortable with my body, with expressing myself as a sexual being.

When I had been little and dreamed of love, it had looked like this.

Yet, other times, it felt like a façade. I felt the cold claws of self-doubt coil around my ankles as they tried to pull me back into darkness.

I noticed the strong reemergence of a trend I'd noticed throughout my entire life: The more I achieved my dreams, the harder I worked to destroy my happiness. I was always moving forward, rising even, while I still knew I was simultaneously imploding.

In those moments, I lashed out at Sam. I cried uncontrollably, and struggled to articulate why I was hurting.

In those moments – when I was at war with myself – I was angry that he only saw a person who looked just the same as any other person, but who was acting utterly irrational for no reason at all.

***

When things were going my way, I always waited for the ball to drop.

"I'm always right about these intuitions," I said to my friend.

"No, you're not," she said. "You just always assume the worst and only notice when you're right."

I was deeply in love with Sam, and he told me he felt the way; I was convinced something had to go wrong, and soon.

Sam was allergic to peanuts, and whenever I didn't hear from him, I was convinced that he had died because of me.

One morning, I could not reach him. My body tensed, and I began pacing around my apartment. I called him again and sent his roommate, a mutual friend, a text asking if she could confirm his vitality.

While I waited to hear back, my mind rewound until I reached the night before when, after studying together in the library, he dropped me off in front of my house. I lived at the top of a little hill. It was the heart of December and the road was glistening with black ice. He put his car in park, and we sat for a moment, grateful to the brakes in his car for protecting us from the treacherous pulls of gravity.

I put my hand on his thigh and felt the hot air flee from the vents and bounce off my skin. We kissed fiercely, but quickly, and then said goodnight; too early in the relationship to say, "I love you."

I walked into my apartment feeling content.

But, then, this next morning, when I did not hear from him at the hour I usually did, I panicked. This was all too good to be true; the time had finally come for something to go terribly wrong.

Shaking with fear, I found of my roommates.

"I think he must be dead," I said. "He must have died from me having a trace of peanuts in my mouth."

"Did you eat peanuts?" she asked.

"Well, no," I responded after mentally checking each food item in each meal from the previous day.

"Then I think you're fine," she said.

Yet, I could not help but think about the far-reaching journeys of the traces of peanuts; those perilous little particles that could be hiding anywhere from packaged foods to restaurant plates to the sponge in my sink that had washed the forks in my drawer. All roads lead to Rome and so much saliva is exchanged when you're in love; exchanged in cavernous mouths so close to a rigid yet delicate throat that could close at any moment because of me.

***

I loved Sam so much that he felt like a part of me; or maybe more I felt like I became a part of him. I lived in an old Victorian house in Providence. My bedroom was just off the checkerboard-floored kitchen, and had beige carpeting and unintentionally off-white walls. We slept on a box spring and mattress stacked on the floor.

At night, we entwined our arms and legs before we fell asleep. He would always fall asleep almost instantly, and I would stay up hours longer. I would silently lie in my place, listening to his steady breathing. As the minutes passed, I would eventually reach a point where I wanted to move away; I wanted to curl up into a ball that contained only me. I would slowly extract what was mine from our entanglement of limbs and gently move to my own corner of the bed. But, I always kept the fingertips of one hand on his shoulder, or my toes just grazing his ankle.

So long as I fall asleep still touching him, this will not be the night I lose love, I told myself.

There I was, practicing magical thinking, like I had as a child.

I knew that as a child this belief was rooted in overwhelming anxiety and dread, and I knew the same could be applied to my current practice.

I believed, regardless; it made the future feel as it it wasn't as utterly out of my control.

{ 36 }

Mental Illness need not be a Bitter Pill to Swallow, So I Say

I was recently at a dinner with two friends, when we began discussing mental illness and mental health treatment.

All three of us have openly had periods of struggle with both depression and anxiety, but we all had very different takes on treatment, particularly in regards to antidepressants.

"I wouldn't go on them," said the first friend.

"I would go on them, but just until I feel better," said the second.

My take was the opposite: I have been taking them on and off my entire life, and since deciding to take them consistently nearly three years ago, my life has turned around. I plan to be on them forever.

Conversations like this are not uncommon. When it comes to mental health issues, opinions are often polarized and strongly held.

I understand that antidepressants are not for everyone; many people are fortunate in not suffering from mental illness, and even many of those who do would prefer to have medication be their last resort.

For me, medication is a part of a more comprehensive treatment plan to avoid falling back into the throes of the major depression that I know always lingers beneath the surface of my delicately balanced equilibrium.

I remember what it feels like to be unwell.

For as far as my memory extends, I recall always feeling a haunting sadness, a darkness that seemed ever-present, as if it lived in my marrow.

Of course, there were times when the depression was more prevalent than others, but – nonetheless - it was always there.

I compare the onset of a particularly heavy spell of depression to a thick fog that moved through my veins and took refuge in my skeletal cavity; I felt weighed down and trapped, a hostage to my own mind.

I remember days, weeks and months where it felt like I was separated from life by a sheet of Plexiglas; I could see what was going on and (mostly) keep up with the world, but everything felt muffled and blurry. The worst depression is not sadness; it is numbness, a haunting apathy and hopelessness. When you fall to that place, it is nothing except empty darkness.

Though I could always feel it, my depression was not always easy to see from the outside. To a maniacal degree, I always pushed myself to excel.

I was high school valedictorian. I was class president. I had many friends. I graduated from Brown University. I held several jobs and showed up and did my work.

Perhaps, on paper, I don't match the stereotypical image of what it looks like to have a mental illness. Yet without a doubt, I know I am mentally ill.

Yes, that's right: I am mentally ill.

I am not sad. I am not going through a phase that I will outgrow; I have major depressive disorder. No matter how happy I am, how many of my dreams I achieve, I know I will always have depression. I do not mean that to be defeatist, I mean it to be pragmatic. My depression is manageable. If I take antidepressants, go to therapy, exercise and abstain from drugs and alcohol, then I am not only able to function, I am able to thrive.

But, on the flipside, if I do not pay attention to my mental health, if I do not do what I need to do, I am aware of where my emotional health can go. Again: It is a very dark place.

I know because I have been there. I spent so many years denying that I was depressed. I spent so many years resisting therapy and medication. I believed they were punitive, or unnecessary. I though it was unfair that I had to go through such measures to create a stable emotional baseline, where most of my friends just naturally found themselves there.

That period of my life was turbulent. It can be defined by suicide attempts and drug and alcohol abuse; by eating disorders and emotionally paralyzing spells of depression; by dysfunctional relationships and general despair. I have had my life commandeered, and almost taken, by my mental illness.

I know so many others have, as well.

Though I am not afraid to admit that I am mentally ill, I understand why people are: Mental illness is still stigmatized. Nationally, we mostly speak about mental illness in the wake of mass shootings, or after suicides. Historically, when people suffered from mental illness, they were shipped off to devastating institutions. As a result, people might worry that they'd lose jobs, friendship or romantic relationships if they were honest about their mental health issues.

Mental illness should not just be spoken about in these contexts. It should be spoken about all of the time.

Mental illness is common: According to the National Alliance on Mental Illness, "One in 5 adults experience a mental health condition every year. One in 17 lives with a serious mental illness such as schizophrenia or bipolar disorder."

One of the worst parts of mental illness is this idea of isolation and silent suffering, the belief that your feelings and behaviors are wrong, that they must be hidden and denied.

The only way we are going to make the mental health system better is if all we all start having honest dialogues about what we, or our loved ones, need to be healthy.

Therapy and medications are not punishments, and they are not luxuries either. For many people, they are necessary for survival - and certainly necessary for having a high quality of life.

Mental illness should be treated like physical illness; there is nothing in it to be ashamed about. You should not have to share it if you are diagnosed, but you should not feel like you have to hide it either.

Everyone who suffers from it experiences diverse symptoms, and everyone will respond differently to varying treatment methods and approaches, as well.

One thing is for certain: Having a mental illness does not make you weak, and it does not make you a bad or dangerous person.

It makes you a person with a unique set of challenges, but they involve obstacles that can be worked through, and - if not completely overcome - then at least controlled.

You can be happy, and you can be free, but it takes work, commitment and self-honesty.

As a society, it takes reform; we need increased access to affordable quality mental health care, and we need to change the way we perceive and approach mental illness and mental health treatment.

As we approach a presidential election, when we often talk about health care and reform of the health industry, in general, we need to make mental health care a prominent part of that conversation.

We have come too far to have people silently suffering. We have come too far to have people feel alone.

I hope that conversations like the one I had with my friends become more common; that – even if uncomfortable initially – mental illness becomes a conversation that can be had at a dinner table.

Change can only come once taboo is removed; progress can only be made once people feel comfortable being honest.

{ 37 }

Ledge

I stood on the balcony of Sam's family's apartment in Miami. It was my senior spring break, and I'd spent the weekend going from fancy dinners to techno concerts, from nightclubs to strip clubs. I had been partying for days on end, and the steady intake of alcohol and drugs was beginning to take its toll.

Earlier that night, at the Passover Seder on their roof, I had promised myself I would drink carefully and with restraint.

The promise was quickly broken. I had a glass of wine, and I felt better, so then I had another, and then I had another. I felt depleted, and the alcohol made me feel revitalized.

Until it didn't.

Almost as soon as dinner ended, I started crying, and I could not stop, no matter how hard I tried. I wasn't exactly sure where the tears were coming from, but I almost believed that if I kept crying until there were no more tears, this great sadness inside me might escape, as well.

But, as the tears kept coming, I began to feel worse and worse as my intoxication further set in. I felt angry, and lashed out at those around me.

Then, I felt numb.

This is my Senior Spring Break, I thought. *This week is supposed to be lighthearted fun. Why is nothing ever how I imagine it to be?*

Instead, I was alone on the balcony contemplating taking my own life. I put my hands on the railing. I gripped it tightly as I lifted my ankles so just my toes were on the ground. My body tensed and my palms were sweating; every cell of my being could tell what my mind wanted to do, and my physical self was resisting. Yet, in my mind, I knew how easy it would be to push my weight off the ground and soar over the railing. I was well aware of how quickly it could all happen; how it would only take a few excruciating seconds before it would all be over.

I wanted to die. I felt so miserable I was almost certain I could never return to stability, let alone happiness.

Even if I do snap out of it, I'll just be waiting for the next spell of despair to conquer my mind.

In this moment, as I plotted to bring about my own end, all I could think about was whether I would splatter or shatter upon impact with the ground hundreds of feet below. I knew the former made more sense, but I imagined myself hitting the ground like a porcelain doll. I felt so lifeless and full of air; an empty vessel that looked like a human, but no longer really was alive.

Now, I thought. *Now is the time.*

I knew I was drunk enough to do it. I knew there would be no question the impact would kill me swiftly.

Then I began to doubt the method.

I haven't written anyone letters explaining my decision, I thought. *That would be selfish to leave without saying why, without saying goodbye.*

I reminded myself that someone was sure to see me do it; and someone else would have to remove my body from the pavement.

It felt so unfair to traumatize these strangers.

So I gave myself time.

If you still feel this way in the morning, then you can do it.

***

In the morning, I awoke next to Sam; I was instantly disturbed by my breakdown the night before.

I no longer felt quite so hopeless. I decided I would let myself live.

I was troubled by the thoughts I'd had the night before, but I pushed them to the back of my mind. To linger within those thoughts made me fear they might come back too soon.

It was much more simple to go about as though they had never crossed my mind; as though I hadn't thought them many times before.

{ 38 }

The Graduate

I didn't graduate from Brown anywhere near the top of my class; I didn't leave with honors, or having written a thesis. I didn't have a fancy job lined up, or any job lined up, at all.

In comparison to my high school graduation, I felt subpar.

What I had accomplished in college, was something I never could have imagined four years earlier when I was leaving my little high school world: I was in love. I had a boyfriend. I was more secure in my sexuality. I had a real relationship.

I knew I was moving to New York. I was going to live with Jonny in an apartment his parents had bought him in SoHo.

Sam would also be in the City for the summer.

But, already, I began to think about the fall. Sam was the year below me, and at the end of the summer, he would return to Brown. I had a sinking feeling he wouldn't want to be in a long distance relationship.

I didn't have much money saved up; I'd spent four years essentially living off students loans, and soon after graduation, I knew I'd have to start paying those backs.

Even as I smiled in pictures that weekend, a part of me could already feel everything I'd prioritized so swiftly slipping away.

{ 39 }

Unraveling

"Can I turn the light on?" I asked Sam, as we lay in his four-poster bed at his family's apartment on the Upper East Side.

Sam ignored me, keeping his attention on the episode of *The Real Housewives of Beverly Hills* that he was watching on his laptop.

"Can I turn the light on?" I said it louder this time, attempting to shout over the screaming women in ball gowns who held my boyfriend's gaze.

Sam paused the show, and closed his eyes. He looked rankled; he took an audibly deep breath.

The idea that I could make someone who once loved me so exasperated was both exhilarating and devastating.

A moment passed, and Sam let out a sigh.

"Are you serious?" he asked.

"I want to read," I pleaded.

"It's late and I have to work tomorrow," he now often spoke to me as though I was a child. "Just watch the show and go to bed."

***

Beside me, Sam was fast asleep. His breath moved in and out without the slightest interruption.

I couldn't sleep. I got up from the bed and walked to the living room. Some of his family members were home, but like Sam they were all peacefully asleep. At this hour, in the darkness, the house felt cavernous and the air was still; it felt dead.

In the living room, I sat on a couch and opened my book. Staring at the page, I read the same paragraph over and over. No matter how many times my eyes scanned over those sentences, none of it made any sense. I couldn't retain a word.

I kept trying to reread the sentences. Over and over, I went back to beginning.

If you cannot comprehend the meaning of these simple sentences, then you truly must be going completely insane.

Fuck it.

All I wanted was sleep.

Why can't I just fall asleep like other people?

I knew sleep would not come. It rarely ever did those days.

I walked back to Sam's room and quietly returned my body to his bed.

His tranquil breathing drove me crazy. I'd always been jealous of the way he just closed his eyes and instantly slipped off to dreams. Right then, I wanted nothing more than to shake him until he awoke. I wanted him to suffer from insomnia, too. Everyone wants to share their misery, and I was no exception.

I tossed and turned, and I was certain he was going to wake up soon.

I couldn't take another moment of stirring, so I got back out of bed and I glided across the hall to his sister's childhood room.

Maybe I'll have better luck trying to sleep alone.

After twenty minutes of trying to force myself to surrender to sleep, I gave up.

It's time to try another way.

I went into the bathroom and opened the medicine cabinets. I was trying to find anything over the counter that would knock me it.

If you cannot go to sleep, you must create it.

There was no Benadryl; there was no Nyquil; there was no Dramamine.

I walked back into Sam's room, and went to my suitcase to extract the small baggy filled with Klonopin and Ambien. I had stolen this stash from my sister's pill bottles on top of the fridge when I'd gone home the week before.

I never did do well with moderation, and I'd promised myself I'd stop using both of these a year before.

For a while, I'd kept my promise.

But, that was before the sleep stopped coming on its own.

I have to sleep.

I took an Ambien and a Klonopin, and then I lay back down in bed.

***

Sitting at the desk in an extra bedroom of Jonny's parent's Park Avenue penthouse, I began writing my card to Sam.

I had been staying at Jonny's increasingly frequently to give Sam a break. I felt myself smothering him, but I couldn't help but cling. I feared Sam was on the verge of ending our relationship.

I couldn't bear the thought of another change; everything was changing.

That night was our six-month anniversary.

I hadn't known what to get him.

What do you buy for someone who can buy whatever they want, whenever they want?

I decided a sentimental gift was the answer: A frame filled with pictures of us.

After purchasing a frame at Crate and Barrel downtown, I walked back from SoHo to the top of the Upper East Side. It was raining, and several times I thought of getting on the subway, or hailing a cab, but I just kept walking.

The frame's box became soggy, and I was completely drenched, but I needed to keep walking. It was both punitive and cathartic. I had to finish what I'd started.

Once back at Jonny's, I'd filled the frame with pictures of Sam and I, together at college: Sam standing on a rickety chair to tie a tie around my neck; the two of us drunkenly clinging to each other at a party.

The gift was a plea; I desperately wanted to remind him that we once had fun, that we loved each other, or at least *had* loved each other.

I remembered the night that each picture was taken, and I knew that at least two ended with me starting a drunken fight or spontaneously bursting into tears. At least one of the nights then escalated into a full-blown emotional breakdown. I hoped Sam's memory was not quite so detailed as my own.

As I wrote out the card to Sam, I thought back to all the cards we'd written each other at Brown. I'd toiled over the cards, and he said he'd done the same. I'd always been so nervous about not choosing the right words. People said romance was dead, but our cards had been like love letters from long ago.

I was trying to write another one in that category now, and I wanted it to be the most beautiful one I had written yet. I needed it to be. I was trying to put into words how much I loved Sam.

At first, the words wouldn't come.

Write, I begged myself. *Write something magical.*

My hands began moving, and the ink curved and formed letters, which eventually bled together to make words. I read them over, and they sounded pretty, and their message was sweet.

My stomach dropped.

I could be writing this card to anyone, I thought. *It feels like writing fiction.*

Nothing felt special anymore. I remembered the summer before, when I'd lived in the City and everything felt enchanted. I'd been falling in love with Sam and with the City, and every walk to the coffee shop or ride on the subway felt like an adventure.

The magic that surrounded the City and our relationship was missing these days. I was worried that magic might even be gone, but not just from this one city on the map or from this one boy in my heart; I was worried that my sense of wonder was gone from everything.

I pushed these thoughts aside. I couldn't indulge such dark thoughts, these days, as they came much too often; they were now almost always there.

Instead, I fixed my posture and picked up the glassful of Chardonnay that was calling to me. After swallowing deeply, and almost inhaling the wine, I willed my hand to keep writing. The card seemed to finish itself, and almost as soon as the words were down, I'd forgotten what they were.

I walked to the mirror and practiced how I would smile softly at dinner; how to look like who I used to be.

The face looked wrong, the eyes were sunken and the way the lips curled looked unnatural.

I wondered if I should slap myself. *Would that make my face look how it used to? Would that make me feel more grounded? More real?*

I refrained simply because I was afraid I might leave a mark.

Maybe I'm the only one who can tell I am no longer myself.

***

"Are you sure you don't want to come to the play?" Jonny asked.

We were finishing dinner with his parents in the Theatre District, and they had an extra ticket for the show they were about to see.

"Yeah, I want to see Sam," I, responded, realizing how pathetic the words sounded as they came out. "But, thank you for inviting me."

Jonny looked concerned, but he gave in. He knew how stubborn I could be.

"Call me if you change your mind," he said.

"I will," I said, as I climbed into Jonny's family's black Escalade and went back to the Upper East Side.

***

Sam and I took a cab from the Upper East Side to SoHo. It was pouring, and we were completely quiet on the ride down.

Sam's friends arrived at the restaurant. They used to be my friends too, but recently I felt an invisible wedge; it was like an unspoken distance had appeared from nowhere. All of my interactions with them felt forced and feigned. I wondered if anyone felt that but me?

I only ate crudo and picked at branzino during the meal with Jonny's family, but I lied and said I'd already eaten.

"I'm just going to have a glass of wine," I said.

I proceeded to spend the remainder of the meal pounding glass after glass of Pinot Noir.

Even for me, I realized I was drinking a lot these days.
I wondered if part of my blood might just become permanently alcohol.

I knew the thought should trouble me, but right now, it didn't.

There are worse things in life than needing a little wine everyday, I thought.

As the meal wrapped up, people began discussing what they were going to do with their night.

"I need to go to my high school friend's party at Finale," Sam said to the group.

I knew he was going, but I thought I'd be invited to go, as well.
No invitation came.

"Can I not come?" I asked, quietly.

"I can let you know," Sam said tersely. "It's not like I'm paying for it, so I can't really just bring people along."

Though the logic made sense, I knew the girl whose party was that night was wildly wealthy, and I was convinced that she wouldn't care if I came if Sam just asked.

I also knew that three months ago, he would have wanted me to come.

Deep down, I knew why this was. My excessive drinking and volatile behavior was destroying the relationship.

I was watching it happen, wanting it to stop, but I couldn't. Alcohol was getting me through each day.

On some level, I felt sick; so mentally and emotionally sick. I felt like I was being punished for my sickness; a sickness I refused to admit I had.

I knew I was being impossible, but I believed if someone truly loved you, they would figure out a way to reach you.

The sadness over feeling rejected quickly transitioned to anger.
It must have shown on my face.

"I'll let you know," he said, rather unconvincingly.

I'm not stupid, and I won't be treated as such, I thought. *He won't even be honest with me.*

"Don't even bother," I snapped, feeling the tears shooting from the depths of my darkness toward the outside world. It was pouring rain, and we were moving toward the door to the street.

I was so sick of looking crazy in front of people, so I just bolted out without looking back. It was pouring rain, almost as ferociously as the monsoons had in India, and instantly I felt like a drenched disaster.

The tears came, and they blended with the rain as they slid down my face.

I was embarrassed that I'd freaked out. But, I had to convince myself, I was right; that I was being wronged. If I lost that belief, I'd fall apart.

You're justified, I told myself. *You would have reacted like that even if you weren't drunk.*

I've been feeling so flat lately, like a zombie, I thought. *Feeling sadness and anger is a step up from feeling nothing at all.*

***

I felt liberated having run off into the rain, until I realized that all of my stuff was at Sam's house.

I went back uptown to Sam's, where I shed my wet clothes, and took a warm shower.

When I got out, I realized that I was much drunker than I'd thought. I was wound up; I cursed myself for not being the level of intoxication where you just passed out.

I didn't want to see Sam when he got home; I needed to be in a coma-like state.

Everything will feel better when I wake up, I thought.

Even as I tried to convince myself, I knew it was actually often the opposite.

In the mornings, I often felt ill, and was also sober enough to begin to understand how volatile I'd behaved the night before.

But, I held onto hope. If I slept, maybe I would wake up and no longer be sad. I wanted to wake up and have everything around me be better; I wanted to feel myself again.

Sleep felt even further away than usual. I felt so manic; I had too much energy.

I knew that I needed to make sleep come; it certainly wasn't going to come by itself. I needed to take measures into my own hands.

What can I use? I thought. *How can I sedate my body and my thoughts?*

I saw the bottle of Vicodin that Sam had from getting his wisdom teeth removed.

I'd eyed the bottle before, but I'd been trying to be better about limiting my secret recreational ingestion of prescription pills.

But, at that moment, I feared what would happen as the alcohol continued to sink in; it felt like sadness expanded through my blood and then totally took over my mind.

Just one, I thought, as I opened the bottle of Vicodin and popped a pill into my mouth.

As I lay down on Sam's bed, I felt a calmness wash over my body; my mind was finally still. It was just like floating; I felt so peaceful.

Twenty minutes later, the feeling began to lightly fade, so I took another pill.

Floating.

Half an hour later, I felt an imminent fading again, so I took a third.

Floating.

Twenty minutes later, I still felt quite high, but I was frightened by the idea of this high ending. I took a fourth, and waited for the floating feeling to intensify.

It didn't; darkness took over instead.

***

In the morning, I woke up feeling so nauseous I could hardly move. Sam was lying next to me, and I was petrified I might vomit in the bed.

I was shocked I hadn't thrown up in my sleep.

I finally mustered the strength to drag myself to the bathroom, where I made myself throw up.

I felt poisoned.

When I got back to bed, Sam stirred and then awoke.

If I apologize, then that means I'm admitting I'm wrong. I hate giving up that power.

But, I knew I had to. I knew I was losing my ability to handle situations like an adult, and I wanted to save face.

"I'm sorry for last night," I said, a line which was becoming quite familiar.

"It's fine," he said, dryly. "Let's just forget about it."

***

Sam's parents took us to brunch at Nougatine in Columbus Circle.

We sat outside beside the globe sculpture. The sun was beating down, and I was mildly convinced I was slowly dying.

I couldn't keep up with the conversation; everything just felt like white noise. I tried to focus, but couldn't.

I excused myself from the table and walked normally to the bathroom. Most of my actions no felt like acting; it always felt like I was trying to impersonate my former self.

Once inside, I knelt on the floor and secretly heaved tuna tartare into the chilly porcelain toilet.

Who have I become?

{ 40 }

The Last Party

I arrived at Sam's best friend's lavish birthday party at the NoMad Hotel, already annoyed. Sam had never messaged me to say I should come meet him, as he said he would.

Instead of taking the hint and making other plans, I'd stubbornly decided that there was no way I was missing the party. I'd spent the early evening drinking alone while waiting for my phone to buzz.

It didn't, and I couldn't say I was that surprised.

A few days earlier Sam had already told me he felt like it wasn't working.

"We've been fighting so much," he said.

I thought about the fights; how I was always so drunk during the fights.

I could have blamed it on drinking, I thought. *But, then I'd probably have to stop.*

I pushed the thought out of my head.

***

I saw Sam and the birthday boy at the bar. I made my way over to them.

"Hello," I tried to say pleasantly, while detecting the faintest bit of snarl in my own voice.

"You should have come to dinner," exclaimed the birthday boy.

I wasn't invited, I wanted to say, already feeling so angry. Yet, I knew my anger and volatility were the reasons why Sam no longer wanted me around. I felt trapped in the cycle I'd created.

I looked at Sam who appeared to be uncomfortable.

"I'm going to order a drink," I said, smiling.

***

Drink, after drink, after drink.

They went down like water.

I quickly lost count.

I floated on the dance floor happily faded, and the next moment I felt anger.

I was screaming, but I didn't know at whom.

Then there was darkness, and when I came back I was on the street. Someone was restraining me, and all I felt was a gravitational pull toward the bright lights that zoomed by.

The traffic was like a river, and I needed to drown myself.

I pulled toward it; I tried to rip away from the grip on my arm.

"SEAMUS, STOP," a voice screamed, pulling me back.

But, I kept yanking toward the sound of wheels on the ground.

***

The darkness seemed to last forever, but I finally was aware of a thudding in my head.

I opened my eyes, and as light entered my pupils it felt like I was being bashed over the skull with a hammer.

The thudding in my head continued, until I realized it was not the sound of my pulse.

There was a pounding on my door.

Hardly able to move, I checked my phone. It was well after 2 pm.

The screen was full with notifications of people texting me. I could not bring myself to open any of the texts.

I knew something bad happened, but I couldn't remember what.
The pounding on the door wouldn't stop.
I got up and opened it.
Jonny was standing there, petrified.
"I thought you were dead," he said.
"No," I replied meekly. "I'm still alive."
"Do you remember anything?"
"Not really," I said.
"You tried to run in front of cars, and then you were brought back here, and you had a complete breakdown."
"I'm sorry," I said.
I was on the verge of tears, but even the act of crying felt like it would take too much effort.
"I woke up to you coming into my room and swallowing a handful of sleeping pills in the middle of the night," Jonny continued, on the verge of tears himself. "You swore you didn't take any, but so many are missing. I shouldn't have let you go to sleep."
"I'm sorry," I said. "I really don't know what to do anymore."
"You can't do that again," Jonny said. "Or I'll have to kick you out. Not because I'm mad at you, but I can't watch you do that to yourself. I can't let you kill yourself."

***

The taxi uptown cost $40, and several times I thought I was going to heave to vomit out the window.
I needed to get to Sam's; it was all I could think about. I wanted to kick myself for not ending this relationship with elegance.
I was so frustrated and embarrassed that I was pinching my own arms. I felt like a child, wanting so badly to be able to undo what I had done. I was embarrassed by my temper tantrums, and yet kept having them, relying on them more and more to express myself.
My body felt so poisoned that I was shaking uncontrollably.
When, I made it to Sam's, and walked into the lobby, I realized this would probably be the last time I ever entered the building.
In my head, I said my goodbyes.

I walked through the lobby with the murals on the wall, and said hello to the doormen who all knew me by name.

I got into the elevator, which was old-fashioned and had to be operated by one of the doormen.

"How are you today?" he said smiling.

"I'm good!" I lied, surprised at how naturally it came out; how easily I could momentarily fake happiness even now.

***

Sam greeted me coldly when the door opened. He instantly guided me into his bedroom. We sat far apart from each other on the bed. He would hardly even look at me.

"You wanted to talk?" Sam barked, not looking up.

"I'm sorry," I said, my voice small. "I don't even remember what happened."

"You humiliated me in front of my friends," he said. "You were too drunk to keep coming out with us, and I was sending you home and you just kept screaming that I should go fuck myself."

"I'm sorry, I don't remember that at all," I said, crying. "And then I tried to hurt myself and I barely remember that either."

Sam looked up, and I watched the defensiveness leave his face. He could see that I was hurting, and the anger he had built up visibly washed away.

For a moment, I felt relieved.

Then, I realized the look on his face was devastating: No one wants to be pitied by their boyfriend.

I felt devoid of pride.

I'd just almost killed myself after publicly falling apart at a party. I'd had a complete breakdown.

Like a normal person, I wanted to be able to just calmly say, '*I don't think this is working.*' I wanted to be able to have a normal conversation.

But, this wasn't a normal breakup. None of my behaviors were normal anymore.

This wasn't something that was 'not working;' even I knew that wasn't what had unfolded. I was a man struggling with mental illness and a substance abuse disorder. I was disintegrating.

Any relationship I was in couldn't have worked. Sam was not perfect, but deep down I knew that everything was falling apart because I was completely fucked up. I was out of my mind.

All of this was in my head, but none of those words came out of my mouth.

Though I was beating myself up in my head, I was too proud to admit I was disaster. I was scared of what I might have to do when I said those words aloud.

"Are you even happy in this anymore?" Sam asked.

"No," I responded, being honest for the first time in a long time.

What I didn't say was that it wasn't just the relationship in which I was unhappy; it was everything, everyday.

"Okay," Sam said, gently. "I think we need to both just work on being happy."

I could tell him I need to go to rehab. I could tell him I can't control myself when I drink. I could convince him that these tantrums and breakdowns aren't actually who I am.

But, I wasn't ready to do make that commitment to change; Sam might still say we were done even if I did.

I had to allow him to separate himself from me, instead.

I put my head on Sam's lap, and remembered the year where I told myself that being in this position was what would bring me happiness; I thought back to the moments where I had felt at peace with him. The years of my life where all I'd dreamt of was love, flashed before my eyes.

I sat up and tried to kiss him one last time. Maybe I might find some answer in this last kiss; maybe it would give me the courage to be honest.

Sam stopped me. He held my head gently between his two hands and kissed me on the forehead, instead.

There was such compassion in the kiss, but it wasn't romantic; it felt like a parent trying to comfort their disturbed child.

I sat with Sam in silence. I knew that once we stood, I might never speak to him again.

I knew I was in the wrong, but I was still furious at him for not wanting to save me; for not being able to save me.

"Okay, I have stuff I need to do for work," Sam eventually said, softly. His voice was the strangest hybrid of strain and relief.

I rose and Sam walked me to the elevator and pushed the button.

The elevator came so quickly. I hugged him passively, and then turned and stepped in.

"Call me, if you ever need to talk or want to hang out," he said, sadly. "I love you."

The elevator doors closed between us.

Immediately, I began convincing myself I was the victim. It was the only way I knew to get through.

{ 41 }

Help

I entered the office building of my new therapist, Kevin, on Broadway near the Flatiron building.

He had come highly recommended by the mother of one of my best friends.

"He's a therapist who focuses on drinking issues in gay men," she had told me.

His office was simple and pleasant. The room was bright and without distractions.

"So what's going on?" Kevin asked.

Don't lie to this one, I thought. *Maybe he can really help you.*

I told him everything. I spilled about my history with drinking, about my suicide attempts, about my breakdown and my subsequent breakup.

"Okay," he said calmly. "Are you still drinking?"

"No," I said. "I haven't had a drink since that night."

"Drugs?"

"No."

"Let's keep it that way," he says. "For now at least."

***

The summer unfolded faster than I could handle.

I'd started a new job, teaching formerly incarcerated men and women how to use computers, create resumes and apply for jobs.

I went into work and pretended I had my own shit figured out. In my head I felt like a farce for persuading my students they should listen to me.

I'm a disaster.

At night, I thought about quitting my job and just going to rehab. *I'll pick out my own this time. I'll find one I actually like.*

But, I didn't.

Going to rehab meant I would never be able to drink again.

I thought I might still have a shot at achieving moderation.

I read blogs about becoming a moderate drinker; I was obsessed.

On the internet, you can always find the answer that you want; there is always someone who is willing to give it.

I believed I was just taking some time off to reevaluate how I could finally learn to drink healthily. I thought this would be the time I learned how to drink like everyone else.

***

"I think I'm ready to try alcohol again," I told Kevin at his office, several appointments later.

A month had passed of skipping parties.

It had been a month of feeling like everyone was watching me; it seemed like everyone was worried about me but afraid to say anything.

The month had gone by slowly; it had been flat and sad. I'd spent most of my time in bed, or wandering the streets not sure where I was going. I thought about Sam, and the loss of the relationship and it hurt; it hurt like nothing I had ever felt.

I already hated myself, so I dealt with the new pain by convincing myself I hated Sam. If I allowed that anger to move inward, I was terrified of what I might do.

I felt so empty, and as always, I thought the solution might be found in glasses of wine, extravagant parties or sex.

"Are you sure you're ready?" Kevin asked.

"Yes," I said. "I can't take another day of punishing myself."

"Well, if you're going to try again, we need to at least make some rules."

"Fine."

"Let's start with when you'll drink," he said. "Weekends?"

"Yeah," I said. "I'll stick to weekends."

"Ok," he said, beginning to write down our agreement on a piece of paper. "So Friday and Saturday drinking only."

"And Thursday," I said. "All of my friends go out on Thursdays."

He looked at me as though he had something he wanted to say.

"I'm only 22," I said.

"Fine," he said. "How many drinks each night? One?"

"Three," I said, trying to think if I've ever only had three drinks in one night.

"Three is a lot," he said.

"Not if it's spread out over a whole night."

"Alright, fine," he said. "Let's give it a try."

***

"I'm going to try drinking again," I told Jonny that night. We were going to our friend's house in the Hamptons for the weekend.

"Are you sure?" he said.

"My therapist said it's okay," I informed him. "We've talked about it a lot, and he thinks I'm ready to drink carefully."

"Ok, I guess," he said not convinced.

I opened a bottle of wine and poured two glasses. Jonny took, one, hesitating.

I'd already had a beer, but he didn't have to know.

***

At the end of the weekend, on the Jitney ride back to the City, I felt like I was dying. I convinced myself that I was on the verge of an aneurysm.

I'm fine, I thought to myself, after each deep breath. *My body just isn't used to being this hungover anymore.*

The night before in the Hamptons, we had pounded shots. I had blacked out the night before that, as well, but I'd had fun. We danced, and took pictures and laughed. I met new people who felt like old friends after sharing round after round of drinks.

Nothing bad had happened.

That's all that matters.

Yet, this feeling of being poisoned - the knowledge that it would take days before I felt fully recovered ... I wasn't sure how much longer I could handle it.

I was almost ready to tell everyone that I couldn't drink anymore. I wanted to ask them not to let me when I was with them.

But, when I looked around the bus at my passed-out friends, their Gatorades in their laps, I realized they were all hungover, too.

It's normal, I told myself. *We just had a wild weekend.*

***

When I went back to Kevin that Wednesday, I didn't tell him about blacking out in the Hamptons, and I didn't tell him that I drank several glasses of wine the night before at a friend's birthday dinner.

I noticed a change within myself. My mind was tired.

It was becoming harder and harder to convince myself that these were just isolated incidents. I kept wanting to believe they were just moments that unfortunately popped up during my first week of returning to drinking, but I couldn't.

"How is it going?" he asked.

"Good!" I forced out.

"Did you try drinking?"

"Yes," I said. "It was fine."

The ease with which I could lie, and how convincing my lies sounded, it never failed to blow me away.

"Are you drinking a glass of water between each drink?"

"Yes."

"Are you finding it hard to control yourself?"

"A little," I said. "But, I'm so much more mindful now."

"Are you okay?" he asked.

"Yes," I said, in a way that made me feel so pathetically resistant to the truth.

***

On a Friday night a few weeks later, I stood outside of the current 'it' bar, Acme, with a group of my friends. We were waiting to be let in, but had been asked to step to the side.

"C'mon," Jonny said to the pompous doorman. "We're going to spend a lot of money inside."

"Give it a few," the bouncer replied, dismissively.

There were a million other bars in the city where we could just walk in. We could have left so easily, but we didn't.

We stood waiting in our spots, desperate yet certain we'd be let in.

We were unwilling to accept defeat.

"Go ahead," the doorman finally said. Some invisible incident had finally made him decide that we appeared attractive enough, or wealthy enough – or perhaps the bar was empty enough – that we are acceptable to be allowed inside.

We walked down the stairs and into the basement hallway that led to the speakeasy. We felt so glorious in our victory.

We threw open the door to the bar, ready to party.

A party there was not.

The bar was nearly empty; it was essentially dead.

"Seriously?" I asked. "He just made us wait for this?"

But, now we were here. We had just waited so long. We had to at least have one drink.

Like most venues of this exclusive social caliber, we quickly realized we were not going to have any fun.

Unless we got shitfaced.

"Let's drink?" someone said, and we were like dogs lets loose upon a buffet.

We ordered round after round of the tiny $15 cocktails. My friends took turns charging the rounds of overpriced drinks to AmEx's that were attached to their parents' bank account.

We were all pounding drinks. They were so fancy – they used egg whites and hibiscus, elderflower and aloe – and went completely unappreciated; we knocked them down as though they were $2 tequila shots.

We sat in a booth, and I quickly grew drowsy.

When my friend turned her head I gulped her glass of rosé. When she turned back toward me, I lay in her lap and began to fall asleep.

***

I opened my eyes and was blinded by the intense light that streamed though my floor to ceiling window, which took up an entire wall in my bedroom.

The apartment, which was owned by Jonny's parents, was a young person's dream: If you drilled a hole directly through my ceiling, and kept going for five or six floors, you would emerge in Justin Timberlake's living room; and somewhere along the way you would have passed through the New York dwelling of a British princess and the pied-à-terres of other unfathomably wealthy people from all around the world.

This was the lifestyle I'd dreamt of as a little kid. This is what I'd wanted since I was that small child counting change on the floor; I moved in circles of affluence and influence.

Life in the fast lane.

I'd thought all of this would make me happy.

But, I was miserable; I allowed myself to accept that I was absolutely fucking miserable.

My bed faced a full wall bookshelf with a built-in rolling ladder. The painting above my bed had been hung by a fashionable interior decorator, who had also recommended the bedframe and bedding color scheme that I then used her interior decorator discount to purchase.

The room was pristine. From the rays of sun that reflected off the dark treated hardwood floors, to the fully stocked rows of books that were all pulled out so their spines perfectly lined up with each other, everything in the room was perfectly in place.

I felt like I was on a set; I was supposed to be playing my part, but I had forgotten all of my lines.

I quickly scrolled through my texts to make sure I had not drunkenly messaged Sam.

I breathed a sigh of relief when I realized I hadn't. I let myself relax. I kept reading through my messages.

I grimaced as I noticed a text I had sent a boy who I hardly knew.

"Where are you?" I had asked him at 2 am.

"Who is this?" he responded at 2:15.

I began trying to piece together the rest of the night.

How did I get home?

All I wanted was to remember what happened, but I couldn't; a continuous memory just wouldn't form.

There were flashes of visions; there were brief clips of sound.

Being shaken awake.

Being in a cab with my friend.

Being shaken awake again.

The feeling of anger.

The relief of lashing out.

Then, there was nothing more I could recall.

I tried calling my friend whose face I remembered seeing in the taxi.

She didn't answer.

Shit, she's furious at me.

I was falling down a black hole of 'what ifs'; I was snaking through a shame spiral.

What horrible things did I say to her?

What did I do?

I needed to talk to someone. I tried to think of who would be awake.

My dad.

I can't tell him, I thought. *What if I change my mind? He'll hold me to it.*

"I have to stop drinking," I sobbed aloud to no one but myself. "I can't do this anymore."

Suddenly, I realized I was serious this time; this wasn't some act.

Something in me knew that I would actually be found dead soon if I didn't stop.

Whether it is from getting hit by a car, falling into the subway tracks, dying of alcohol poisoning or being murdered, something bad was going to happen to me; it felt unavoidable.

I couldn't control myself anymore. I never could when it came it alcohol.

I have to stop drinking; I have to let it go.

In that moment, I could almost visualize the future I'd imagined for myself: I saw glasses of champagne after getting engaged, and 'day drunk' trips to vineyards; I saw myself meeting potential suitors for cocktails, and buying some beautiful stranger shots at a bars; I saw myself hitting on someone with no fear, and dancing without a care in the world until 6 am.

But, then I saw the truth; I put to words this reality I'd always known, but never wanted to believe.

Those situations were fake, for me at least.

What's the point of having champagne after getting engaged if it means getting in a drunken fight four hours later?

What's the point of buying someone shots at a bar, if I'm going to not remember – or even worse, regret – sleeping with them the next morning?

Dancing until 6 am, kept awake by a drug, doesn't mean I don't have any cares; it means that in that moment I bury them, and when I wake up they'll be back nagging louder than ever.

And what's the point of any of this, knowing this my truth: That one night I'll have one drink too many, and not be able to come back. It won't be something that can be cured with Advil, Gatorade, self-induced vomiting, IVs or naps; it will be death; stone cold, final, no-coming-back-from-it death.

I will die chasing intoxication; I will die being intoxicated.

It will not be glamorous; it will be gruesome. It will be failed organs; it will be poisoning; it will be me, but not me, a cold dead corpse covered in vomit, maybe even blood.

I'd always believed there was a beauty in tragedy; I'd been convinced I attracted people with my streak of madness.

Sure, I told myself, *your existence can continue to be tragic, but not for long.*

The end will be tragic, but not magically so; it will be tragic because it will be such a waste.

"He had so much going for him, but he never could shake the darkness; that need to get and be fucked up."

They'll whisper such things at my funeral. Then I'll become a memory, then an allegory, and finally a statistic.

But, this doesn't have to be.

I picked up the phone one last time, and I dialed the phone number that sat so close to my heart.

A deep voice answered.

"Dad," I managed to get out.

"Seamus. What's wrong?"

"I'm an alcoholic," I said. "I can't do this anymore."

"I've been waiting for this call for years."

***

"Did you drink this week?" Kevin asked; he asked every week since I'd started going.

No," I answered confidently for the eighth week in a row.

"Did you want to?"

"No," I said. "I'm really over it."

"You know," he said, much softer than usual. "When you first said you were quitting. I didn't think you would last a week."

"I knew I would," I said.

"I'm glad I was wrong," he replied.

"Me too."

"What changed this time?"

"I'd never had that reaction before," I said. "It was the first time I really realized how easy it would be to die."

"Are you worried that you'll lose the drive?" he asked. "That as you get further out from this event, you might start second-guessing whether you have to totally abstain?"

"No, I'm not worried," I spurted out quickly, before taking a moment to pause and think.

"Even though that's been your pattern?"

"Yeah," I said. "This time is different."

"Why?"

Why not? I thought. *What had drinking gotten me? Hospitalizations. Breakups. Fights. Depression. Nausea.*

What was left for me in the bottle? Loss. Misery. Loneliness. Death.

"I wasn't done before," I said. "I don't think I have a choice anymore."

"Why now, though?"

"I felt death that morning," I said. "And it didn't feel far. I can't explain it, but I could feel death."

"What do you think got you there?"

"I've been beating myself up over everything I've lost," I said. "I've lost a person I was in love with, countless friendships, and years at Brown – a place I'd believed was truly magical – that I'll never be able to get back."

"Are you angry?"

"Yes. I'm angry at almost everyone I know," I said, starting to choke up. "But, I'm not stupid, I know it's because I'm angry at myself."

"Do you believe you'll be okay?" he asked.

"Yes, because I want to be alive," I said. "If I don't stop drinking, I'll die. It's become so simple, suddenly. I'm without a choice."

"You always will have the choice to back," he said, warily.

"Well, I've made the choice," I said. "I choose to stop drinking because I choose to live."

{ 42 }

After the Party is Over: Finding Myself in Sobriety

Three years ago today, I stopped drinking.

Yesterday, I spoke to my dad – who is also in recovery – about the upcoming anniversary. He wanted to share something someone once told him.

"When you stop drinking, it won't solve your problems," he said. "But you'll be able to know your real problems, and not just the ones you're creating for yourself."

I couldn't agree more.

Three years ago, when I stopped drinking, I knew I had to; if I didn't I was certain I was going to die.

For nearly a decade, my life had, in many ways, been defined by my tumultuous relationship with alcohol. There were hospitalizations, and rehabilitations; there were relationships ruined, and dreams depleted; there were increasingly frightening – and common – blackouts, and days spent in bed miserably recovering from the night before.

Yet, throughout this, I convinced myself that alcohol was what made me happy; what made my life a little less meaningless. I really believed that the intoxicated version of myself was my true being; the sober person that I left behind felt so sad and deflated, so cautious and needy. I didn't believe I was truly happy, but I believed that with alcohol, I was the happiest I could possibly be. I was more than willing to accept the side effects that came with that consumption.

Of course, none of it makes any sense. As a drunken person, I was verbally aggressive; I said mean things to get my way, and in the moment didn't care who I hurt. I was insecure, and I sought emotional and sexual validation. I cried, often; and woke up each morning having done or said at least one thing that I regretted.

If someone was mad at me, or when something bad happened, I always blamed it on the alcohol.

I didn't mean the nasty thing I said, I was drunk.

I didn't actually want to hurt myself; I just had too much to drink.

I know I could have died, but I didn't, and moving forward I'll drink less.

Those excuses (mostly) worked, and I was able to keep drinking to excess. But, I didn't 'get away with it' because I was so much smarter than everyone else (like I thought) or because my drinking habits were more normal than people were acknowledging (like I truly believed.) I got away with it, because at a certain point, people didn't really know what else they could do. You can't help someone who doesn't want to help themself, so they were stuck watching a car crash; some looked away, others ran away and still more watched, holding their breath, hoping that I might come out alive.

At the end of my drinking career, when I realized that I'd lost everything that mattered to me – joy for life, honest relationships, compassion and self-love – I gave up alcohol.

After more failed attempts at quitting than I can event count, this time it worked. I don't think it was because I hit 'rock bottom.' I think I finally opened my eyes and saw how much more darkness lay beneath me; that perhaps there wasn't a true rock bottom and for a person with such a streak of self-destruction, I would always be able to find a new way to hurt myself a little more.

I didn't want that, I realized; I wanted to be happy, or at least to try to be. I wanted to be functional and reliable, and kind. I hadn't been any of things for many years.

In early sobriety, what I found out quickly was another piece of wisdom my dad had tried to impart onto me a year and a half before when he visited me while I studied abroad in India. At the time, I had a full-blown addiction to Xanax, and I was trying to wean myself off. For days, I could not stop crying; I was blaming my emotional state on being in India and out of my comfort zone.

With a blend of sympathy and tough love he turned to me and gently said what someone had once said to him, a line he had heard many times: "You're finding out the hard way that wherever you go, there you'll be."

Early sobriety in many ways, felt much like my time in India: I was navigating terrain that was so far beyond my comfort zone, where all of my preconceived notions were constantly being proven wrong. I was in a place where the only constant was what I wanted to most escape: Myself.

The initial exhilaration of sobriety, and making such a powerful decision made the first week easy.

Then the novelty faded; I was no longer preoccupied with the announcements that I was making to all of my friends and family. They already knew. My coronation was over, and now it was time to do the hard work. It was time to actually be sober, and not just to be told how strong I was, or how proud people were of me. It was time to not drink for myself.

Like my dad pointed out, sobriety did not mean my problems went away; it meant that they were no longer moving targets darting around as blurs in front of me. They were now perceivable and imminent; issues I had to actually face.

Without alcohol, I no longer felt like my bottom had fallen out, but I still felt quite close to, if not on, the bottom. I thought sobriety would be gleeful, I thought that I would now be 'happy' and more easily fulfilled.

That wasn't the case.

Day after day, I had to wake up and just be sober. I had to accept that I didn't like where my life was, and that it was at that point because of decisions I had made. There were some relationships that weren't salvageable; there were some dreams that would take years to fulfill because I'd spent so long trying to find the easiest way out. I had to get used to the sound of my own voice, and think about what I wanted to say and how I said it, because I could no longer say that I had only said it because I was drunk.

I had to accept that there was still a persistent sadness and self-hatred that had not only been there because I'd been an alcoholic.

I thought back to years earlier, when I'd been at a concert. I'd taken Ecstasy with a group of friends, and as it set in, I just kept wanting more. I took another pill, and though most people I was with felt sufficiently high and wanted to avoid drinking, I was seeking it out.

The combination made me feel like I was floating, and numb and dulled. I felt so close to death, yet present. In that moment, I felt bliss.

In sobriety, thinking back to that moment terrified me. What was it inside of me that sought to destroy my own essence? Why did I feel joy in that moment of danger, when I now felt apathetic and flat in this period of self-nurturing?

Answering questions like that has been the hardest part of sobriety. Hell, I still don't have all the answers; I'm not even close.

Becoming sober wasn't like removing the exterior layer of paint on a wrecked car, and finding that there was a perfect, brand new car beneath; everything that I struggled with was still there. The only difference was that it was now just much more visible without the mask of alcoholism.

Without alcohol, I still found that I had mean thoughts, that I sought validation, and that I sometimes still woke up shrouded in darkness. I realized I could still do all of the same shitty things.

I could still spend days in bed.

I could still have mindless sex to remind myself that I was wanted.

I could still punish myself; I could still eat too little, or too much; I could deprive myself of sleep, or not do the things I love.

I could still keep secrets; I could still be guarded, and emotionally opaque. I could still be scared; I could still be dishonest about the things I wanted, and devastated when they didn't happen how I'd hoped.

I don't want that.

I want to dig in; I want to push myself to feel joy and to feel whole. Whether that comes through antidepressants and therapy, yoga and meditation, writing and conversation, I am willing to try it all.

Not all of my questions are answered, and not all of my problems are solved; my urge to self-destruct has dwindled, but it still chirps in, on occasion.

But, my voice of reason is louder and stronger:

No, you shouldn't drink until you're physically there but mentally gone; in fact you shouldn't drink at all.

No, the world is not ending because something went wrong.

Sure, you can sleep with that person, but do you actually want to? He isn't going to magically add meaning to your life.

No, life is not just a river that you blindly hurl yourself into and see where you end up.

I know that each morning, when I wake up, there is only going to be one person, who will never go away from me, and that person is myself.

Three years ago, the fastest way to deny that reality was to get shitfaced.

Today, I am okay with waking up and sometimes feeling uncertain; I am okay with not always feeling content or whole, or brave or sure.

Three years ago, I was scared. Today, I am not.

Today, I can see my problems, and I'm ready to fight.

Acknowledgments

Thank you to my parents, Sean and Nora Kirst, for never giving up; for raising me to believe in the power of my voice; for forgiving and for loving and for having faith; for always picking up the phone. Thank you to my sister and brother, Sarah and Liam.

Thank you to the friends who stood by me, and to those friends who couldn't; to those who comforted me and to those who confronted me. I learned from you all; you all helped me grow.

Thank you to everyone who encouraged me to share my writing; to those who convinced me it might help others on journeys of their own.

Thank you to the writers before me who shared their stories and created the genre; you've paved the road, and inspired me, and without you this book wouldn't have been possible.

Thank you to Alan Rinzler for developmental editing, Jeremy Harding for copyediting, Sean Kirst for final editing, and Maxwell Stern for designing the cover.

Thank you to everyone who supported my Kickstarter:

Walter, Donna, Lily, Annie and Tally Wick
Sade Zimmerman-Feeley
Susan, Dexter, Mercy, Sam and Honor Paine
Thomas R. Riley.
Jonny Cogut.
Karen Magee-Sauer
Barbara Petranto
Maureen Drescher
Megan Toole
Hillary Marshall

Andrew Ressler
Gabi Zerbib
Lily Gildor
Debra H. Schoening
Henry and Katie Nicolella
Lucy Kissel
Heather Wynkoop
Liz Gordon
Emily Braun
Melanie Deziel
Andrew Bruhn
Will Carter
Tess Ritchie
Kerri Comstock
Madison Utendahl
Darrell Kaminski
Matthew Craner
Jessica Cabe
Nell Brodsky
Nina Mullen
Halsey Cooney
Mary Beth Dooley Horsington
The Mosberg Family
Stefan Idowu-Bello
Meg Kirst Lanza
Bridget Lichtinger
Mary Pat Hartnett
Taylor C Lounsbery
Ted Limpert
Isabel Evans
Kyra Mungia
Grace Gosson
Evan Altman
Nora Rothman
Jesse Zannino
Danielle Reilly
Ralph Rodriguez
Jennie Glass
Kenneth Thompson
Katie Drozynski
Caitlyn Moore

Kate Kennedy
Alicia Suskin-Muniz
Shane Wenzel
Kerry Lynch
Brenda Zhang
Shelby Devitt
Carole Horan
Albert Cua
Jesse Eric Schmidt
Jillian Vaccaro
Jim Roaix
Jesse Frank
Dianna Bell
Matt Klimerman
Zachary Pike
Beth Roaix Mathey
Bailey Pfohl
Rachel Ratchford
Carianne Kirby
Josh Moses
Natalie Zises
Nick Desantis
Michelle Breidenbach
Lily Ricci
Eric Vilas-Boas
Lizzy Landau
Janet Anthony
Elizabeth Woodward
Thea Aguiar
Kevin Pires
Meriam Lobel
Rita Brodfuehrer
Gabriel Vogt
Andrea Whittle
Georgia Cook
Jillian Martynec
Sofia Coon
Max Godnick
Hannah Bogen
Gabi Lewis
Lori Reilly

Robert Goltz
Morgan Palmer
Kyle Svingen
Lucy Schultz
Kimberly Wachtler
Katie Alisberg
Bridget Sauer
Jackson Shaad
Kate Welsh
Samantha Hall
Terri Weaver
Wendy Ginsberg
Dorothy Lutz
Jessie Hornig
Ty Marshall
Katherine Reardon
Raquel Laneri
Jared Davis
Sam Levison
Stephanie Wong
John Frewin
Ben Campbell Rosbrook
Siena Kissel
Sydney Mondry
Brady Caspar
Peter Souter
Alexandra Wardlaw
Teresa Doherty
Phillip Maynard
Lindsay Lamont
Sarah Levy
Nell McMahon
Emily Spinner
Jen Kirst-McDonnell
Theresa Murphy
Allie Healy
Kate Groetzinger
Lateshia Beachum
Lauren Williams
Erin Morris
Russell Nohelty

ABOUT THE AUTHOR

Seamus Kirst has written for *Vice, The Guardian, Refinery29, Advocate.com, The Huffington Post, UpWorthy,* and his personal website, *www.seamuskirst.com.* He currently works as the assistant to socio-political comedian, W. Kamau Bell, and he previously worked at a non-profit focused on criminal justice reform. He lives in Brooklyn with his two cats, Sugar Baby and Bernie Sanders. You can follow him on Twitter and Instagram @SeamusKirst, and by 'liking' his page on Facebook, www.facebook.com/seamuspatrickkirst.

Made in the USA
Middletown, DE
03 February 2017